*magnificent Milky Way complete with satellite trail (top centre), Halley's Comet
(bottom centre) and Jupiter (brightest star far right).* Photo M Cooper

A two-hour exposure of stars trails, looking north at Siding Spring Observatory. Note the stars low in the sky arc around the Northern Celestial Pole while those overhead [to arc around the South Celestial Pole. The haziness is the Milky Way.* Photo GD Thompso

THE AUSTRALIAN GUIDE TO
STARGAZING

GREGG D. THOMPSON

LANSDOWNE

To my father for encouraging my childhood astronomical interests and to my devoted wife Gaylia for so unselfishly assisting my adult endeavours. A special thanks to Roy Duncan for his valuable advice and many stimulating discussions on astronomy and related subjects.

Distributed by New Holland Publishers Pty Ltd
3/2 Aquatic Drive, Frenchs Forest NSW Australia 2086

Published by Lansdowne Publishing Pty Ltd
Level 5, 70 George Street, Sydney NSW 2000, Australia

First published in 1993
Reprinted 1995, 1996

© Copyright: Gregg D. Thompson 1993
© Copyright design: Lansdowne Publishing Pty Ltd 1993

Designed by Kathie Baxter Smith
Printed in Singapore by Kyodo Printing Co. (S'pore) Pte Ltd

National Library of Australia Cataloguing-in-Publication data

Thompson, Gregg D.
The Australian guide to stargazing.

Includes index.
ISBN 1 86302 319 4.

1. Stars — Observer's manuals. 2. Milky Way — Observer's manuals I.
Title.
523.80223

Front cover photograph: The Southern Cross by Akira Fujii
Back cover photograph courtesy of European Southern Observatory

CONTENTS

INTRODUCTION

From the dawn of mankind, we have gazed in awe at the starry heavens. Our ancestors wondered whether the stars might be holes in the night that let the light of heaven pass through. But why did some appear to be fixed stars whilst others appeared to fall from the sky? What made the Moon continuously change its shape and position? And what made the Sun so hot and so bright? To our predecessors, the thought that one day their descendants would actually learn how to reach the stars was simply unimaginable!

Throughout the ages, numerous imaginative theories were conceived to explain heavenly occurrences and these theories have been woven into the folklore of all cultures for millennia. Many survive even today. Only in the last few hundred years, and particularly the last 50, has a clear picture of the universe begun to unfold.

Science is often seen as something mathematical and incomprehensible, when, in fact, it is simply a process of observing and gradually understanding our world, ourselves and everything in the universe. Mathematics is simply a tool used to clearly define what has been observed or needs to be tested. Mathematics is not necessary to participate in science, and it is not used in this book.

Even though scientists have made incredible discoveries about the immensity and complexity of the universe, only a small percentage of people know anything about this knowledge. We not only have discovered extraordinary answers to our ancestors' seemingly unanswerable questions but have asked countless more questions that have produced such mind-boggling discoveries as neutron stars, quasars and gravity lenses that were far beyond the realm of our forefather's wildest imaginations. Our descendants are sure to continue discovering even more exotic astronomical objects and concepts.

Inventions such as the telescope, photography, spacecraft, electronics and computers have produced a treasure trove of tools for modern astronomers. Assisted by engineers and technicians, astronomers have developed ingenious ways to explore the solar system, our galaxy (which contains a thousand billion stars) and millions of other galaxies, out to the edge of the universe and beyond. By developing scientific methodologies and making countless observations with unlimited patience, they have been able to test their theories against reality.

The world's most powerful telescopes are now able to peer across the gulfs of time and space to the very edge of the observable universe, and space probes are continuously sending back images and data from worlds that were once unknown or merely specks of distant light. Many discoveries have been so astounding that scientific fact has become more exciting than even the best of science fiction.

In our joyride through the universe, you will learn all the basics to enable you to go stargazing — how to find the planets, how to identify constellations and where to find star clusters, nebulae and galaxies. Using the information in this book, you will be able to thrill others by quoting exciting facts about the stars when stargazing.

We will go on a sightseeing tour of the planets and then thousands of lightyears from home to see coloured stars, enormous stars and a million suns compressed into a ball! We will view clouds of glowing gas and suns that have exploded their atmospheres into cosmic smoke rings. Our journey through the universe ends millions of years back in time when we view other galaxies containing thousands of billions of stars!

Many of the photographs in this book have been taken by some of the world's leading amateur astrophotographers. Amateur astrophotography has been used to give a realistic impression of what a stargazer might expect to see. Enhanced colour photographs taken by the world's largest telescopes are very impressive but they can mislead beginners who sometimes expect to see such images in a small telescope.

This book aims to make the subject of astronomy easy to understand by using a layperson's terms and by taking the novice, step by step, from simple naked-eye astronomy (ie without optical aid), through binocular observing, and on to telescopic observation of deep space. In order to make all numerical facts easy to remember, they are approximate, being rounded off to the nearest hundred, thousand or million and so on.

The Australian Guide to Stargazing should ignite your imagination and fascination for exploring the greatest of all unknowns — the workings of the universe. I hope that its exquisite beauty will touch your heart and that you will be awe-struck by its immensity and curious about the part human intelligence might play in its evolution.

CHAPTER ONE

AUSTRALIA – A LAND FOR STARGAZING

A ustralia offers the best stargazing opportunities in the world. Unfortunately, light pollution has robbed billions of people in other continents of their view of a natural night sky, but Australia's huge geographical area still provides remote regions to escape city lights.

In comparison to many of the northern hemisphere's major population centres, Australia has much milder weather, facilitating comfortable observing conditions. The predominantly flat and dry land also provides far more cloud-free nights, and only Tasmania has the long summer twilights that greatly limit observing time in Europe and North America.

Australia is very well placed to see the bright, rich centre of the Milky Way directly overhead. Northern hemisphere observers see it poorly, low

Australia's 3.9m Anglo-Australian Telescope, the largest of many large telescopes at Siding Spring Observatory that study the universe.
Photo: GD Thompson

on their southern horizon — if they can see it at all. The southern sky boasts the three brightest stars and the best examples of almost every type of object. Australia also has a superb view of the Clouds of Magellan — two extraordinary galaxies visible to the naked eye that are too far south for northern hemisphere stargazers.

Australia boasts some of the world's largest and finest optical and radio telescopes. Three major facilities on the Newell Highway, in New South Wales, make exciting stopovers. Siding Spring Observatory, near Coonabarabran, houses many large telescopes including the 3.9m (150 inch) Anglo-Australian Telescope (AAT), the 2.2m (90 inch) New Technology Telescope (NTT) and the 1.2m (48 inch) UK Schmidt Telescope. This impressive, high-tech observatory features a splendid visitor's display centre and marvellous views of the magnificent, ancient volcanic remnants of the Warrumbungle National Park.

Just outside Narrabri is the **Australia Telescope Compact Array** (ATCA) — a series of huge mobile radio telescopes that use sophisticated technology to combine the radio images from each telescope to act as if it were pieces of one enormous telescope 6km in diameter. Working at the forefront of astronomical research, these telescopes can link up with others around Australia to further enhance their resolving power. An exhibition centre for visitors provides a colourful understanding of how ATCA is expanding our knowledge of the universe.

South of Coonabarabran is the **Parkes Radio Telescope**. This huge 65m (210ft) dish is one of the world's greatest. It has made numerous discoveries and communicated with distant space probes. Parkes Observatory also has an audiovisual education centre.

Mt Stromlo Observatory, Australia's first major observatory, is situated in the hills close to Canberra. It is open to the public. Many large professional telescopes are housed there. Its largest instrument is a 1.9m (74 inch) reflector telescope.

Other public astronomical facilities well worth visiting are **Perth Observatory**, in the Darling Ranges; and the **Sir Thomas Brisbane Planetarium**, located in Brisbane's Botanical Gardens at Mt Cootha, which has a world class 'Cosmic Skydome', and an observatory. Australia has three other fine planetariums: the **Launceston Planetarium**, in Tasmania, the **University of South Australia Planetarium**, in Adelaide, and the **HV McKay Melbourne Planetarium**, in Melbourne.

CHAPTER TWO

STAR MAPS AND ASTRONOMICAL TERMS

Just as we need a street map to find our way around a city, so do we need maps for the sky. Star maps can show you exactly where an object is located amongst a myriad of stars. It is imperative to purchase a good star atlas if you want to be serious about finding your way around the night sky.

Star atlases for naked-eye stargazing show approximately 6000 stars that can be seen with the naked eye, whereas star atlases for serious telescopic observation can contain many hundreds of thousands of stars, or far more. Novices should avoid atlases with numerous faint stars as they are too detailed for beginners and they can be confusing.

It is also important for beginners to use an atlas that shows a large area of the sky on one map so that it is not too hard to find some bright stars or star patterns that can be easily recognised. *Norton's Star Atlas* or *Wil Tirion's Bright Star Atlas* are excellent atlases to start with and they will always be useful. When using an atlas, be sure to orientate it *exactly* as you see the star patterns in the sky, otherwise it is easy to get confused.

Astronomical Numbers: Extremely large numbers (in the trillions and much larger) are frequently quoted when discussing astronomical facts. To appreciate how large a common astronomical number such as one billion is, imagine an Olympic swimming pool being filled by a tap dripping one drop every second. A dripping tap can fill a bucket surprisingly quickly, however, a billion drops will take nearly 31 years to fill the pool.

Magnitude Brightness Scale: Magnitude is a term used to define the brightness of a star or other object. Each magnitude step is 2.5 times fainter or brighter than the next. The scale is such that a 6th magnitude star is 100 times fainter than a 1st magnitude star.

To give examples, the faintest stars that a healthy naked eye can see in a dark, clear sky is magnitude 6. (An experienced observer with excellent eyesight can usually see to 6.5.) The majority of bright stars in the sky are around magnitude 1 to 0. Stars that are exceptionally bright, such as Sirius, Canopus or Alpha Centauri, or the planets Venus, Mars and Jupiter, are so bright that they have negative (-) magnitudes. That is, Sirius is magnitude

-1.5. Superbright shooting stars (bolides) can be -5 to -10. The Full Moon is -12 while the Sun is -27. Magnitudes that have a minus sign are therefore very bright, while stars around magnitude 3 are of moderate brightness. In light-polluted areas, it is common not to be able to see stars fainter than 4.5 to 5. Common 7 x 50 binoculars will show stars to at least magnitude 9.5, whereas a 10cm telescope easily reaches 12.5 and a 20cm telescope will see to magnitude 14. A good astrophotographer using a 32cm telescope can capture stars of magnitude 19, while the world's largest telescopes can reach magnitude 26.

When astronomers determine the brightness of objects that are not starlike, they mathematically 'integrate' the object's brightness (which is spread over an area) and treat it as if all the light is coming from one starlike point. This is called the *integrated magnitude.* This term is often used for extended objects and it can be misleading. For example, catalogues show large nebulae, globular star clusters or galaxies to have magnitudes that make them appear as if they should be fairly bright objects, however, because their brightness is spread out over an area and not compressed into a star-like point, they are usually much fainter than their integrated magnitude would suggest.

North, South, East and West: It is important to have an idea where these directions are so that when we talk about looking toward the east, for instance, you know where to look. Roughly speaking, east is where the Sun rises in summer and northeast is where it rises in winter. Similarly, west is where the Sun sets in summer and northwest is where it sets in winter. If you look directly eastwards, then south is where your outstretched right arm points and north is where your left arm points.

The South Celestial Pole: Where the Earth's poles point out into space are called the Celestial Poles. The star *Polaris* lies very close to the North Celestial Pole (NCP) but only a faint star called *Sigma Octantis* lies close to the South Celestial Pole (SCP). The NCP lies below the northern horizon from Australia, but we can always see the SCP. It is the same number of degrees above due south as the observer's latitude. For example, for Sydney it is 35° above the southern horizon. All the stars in the southern sky rotate around the SCP.

To find the SCP, locate the Southern Cross. Draw a line through the long axis of the Cross pointing south. Measure 4.5 times the distance between the stars of the long axis of the Cross and you are within 3° of the SCP. Another way to find the SCP is to imagine a line drawn at a tangent to the Pointers (Alpha and Beta Centauri) intersecting the line drawn through the long axis of the Cross. The point where the lines intersect is close to the pole.

Right Ascension and Declination: Just as maps of Earth have longitude and latitude, so does the sky. The equivalent of longitude in the sky is called *Right Ascension* while the term *Declination* is equivalent to latitude.

Locating the South Celestial Pole

Celestial Equator: Just as the sky has poles, it also has a *Celestial Equator*. This is situated directly above the Earth's equator, halfway between the celestial poles. Again, as with the Earth, there are 90° between each Celestial Pole and the Celestial Equator. The Equator is 0° Declination while the poles are 90°.

If we draw a concentric line around the pole at any distance from it, this is a line of *Declination* (Dec). Lines of Declination north of the Equator are given positive (+) numbers up to 90, while those south are given negative (-) numbers. Objects with negative Declination or a low positive Declination will be well placed for observing in Australia. Each degree is divided into 60 minutes. And minutes are divided further into 60 seconds when high precision measurements are required.

Lines of *Right Ascension* (RA) are drawn from pole to pole, just as lines of longitude are on maps of the Earth. The sky is broken up into 24 'hour' zones of RA which relate directly to the Earth's rotation each hour. The 24 hours of RA are divided into 60 minutes and, in turn, each minute is divided into 60 seconds, just as for Declination.

If we know the RA and Dec coordinates of an object, then we can find its exact position in the sky. Let's take an example. Say a comet is at RA 14hr 27m, Dec -41° 56m. Using a star atlas, simply find the hour of RA (14) and then the minutes (27). Run your finger along this line until it crosses the Dec line at -41 degrees and 56 minutes. Where the lines cross is the position of the object. As a fun test, use a simple star atlas or planisphere to see what famous object lies at these coordinates in the northern sky: RA 00hr 40m, Dec +41 00m.

Object Names: Once we start observing Deep Sky objects, star clusters, nebulae and galaxies, we will come across designations such as M4 or NGC 5128. These are catalogue numbers. 'M' stands for *Messier*, a French comet hunter named Charles Messier who, in the 18th century, catalogued a little over 100 objects so that he would not confuse them for comets in his small telescope. He would be amazed to see how his little catalogue has immortalised him today. Because he lived in the northern hemisphere, he could not see our bright, far southern objects so these do not carry an 'M' designation.

'NGC' stands for *New General Catalogue*. This mammoth catalogue was compiled in 1888, originally by Dreyer, to list and describe nearly 8000 known deep sky objects. It was revised and improved by Selentic and Tiff in the 1960s and 1970s. Today there are many other categories of special objects.

Common names such as 'Tarantula Nebula' have been given to outstanding objects by both professional and amateur astronomers. These names tend to describe an object's appearance in descriptive terms as opposed to using dry catalogue numbers. Because there are usually hundreds or thousands of objects in every object class, many of which can look quite similar, common names are only useful for the largest, brightest or most distinctive examples.

Zenith: This is a term given to the region of sky directly overhead. It always has a Declination equal to the observer's latitude. For example, the Zenith Declination for Sydney is -35°.

Culmination: When an object reaches its highest point in the sky it is said to have culminated. When a star passes across a line that joins the celestial poles, it is at its highest point from the horizon, known as its Culmination point.

Ecliptic: This is the path that the Sun appears to take as it travels around the celestial sphere over a year. The Ecliptic extends between 23.5° north and 23.5° south of the Celestial Equator. The Ecliptic lies at the centre of the Zodiac. While the inner planets may stay many degrees away, the outer planets stay close to the Ecliptic.

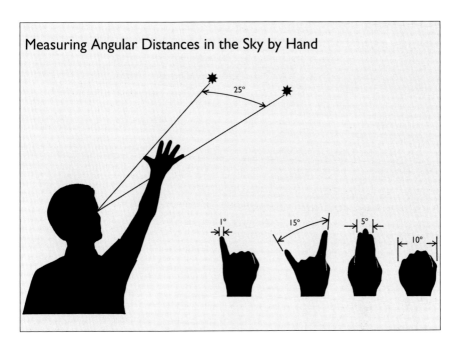

Measuring Angular Distances in the Sky by Hand

Measuring the Sky in Degrees: When astronomers talk about the size of an object in the sky, they measure it in degrees or fractions there of, called minutes. Let's look at some examples. Across the sky dome there are 180° of sky visible if we have a perfect horizon all round. From the horizon to directly overhead is half this — 90°. The distance between the Pointers is 4°, and the Moon and the Sun have a diameter of ½° or 30 arc minutes (30').

A simple way of roughly measuring the sky is to use your outstretched hand at arm's length. From the tip of your thumb to the tip of your little finger is about 25°. A clenched fist at arm's length is about 10° across, while your finger usually covers about 1°.

Diurnal Rotation: This is the apparent movement of the stars across the sky at night caused by the Earth's rotation. Stars in the southern sky rotate around the SCP in increasingly larger circles the further they are away from the pole. The Southern Cross, for instance, never sets in the southern half of Australia because diurnal rotation takes in a large circle around the pole throughout the night, just clearing the southern horizon at its lowest point.

When we look towards the east, the circles have become so large that the stars rise almost vertically from the eastern horizon passing overhead and setting 12 hours later in the west. Stars in the northern sky move along shallow arcs concentric around the NCP, which lies under the horizon by the same number of degrees as the observer's latitude, assuming a perfect horizon.

Star Trail Photography: You can photograph beautiful star trails by using a camera with a 'B' setting for time exposures. Set the camera up firmly so wind won't move it during exposures. Try different exposures (for example, 2min, 15min, 1hr, 3hrs). Direct the camera at different regions of the sky to capture different diurnal arcs. Use high-speed films (400 to 1600 ASA), as they give the best results. Try the widest 'f' stops on your camera lens. To keep dew off the camera lens, use a shelter over the camera that does not intrude on the camera's view, or heat it occasionally with a hair dryer. You will find that the colours of stars will be most pronounced in such pictures.

What Is a Lightyear? A lightyear is a measurement of *distance*, not time. It is simply the distance light can travel in one year. Because distances in the universe are so incredibly large, astronomers had to devise a measure of distance that was very much larger than earthly kilometres otherwise all distances would comprise long cumbersome numbers.

To have the vaguest chance of comprehending huge astronomical distances, consider that light travels at a phenomenal 300,000km every second. Nothing in the universe can travel faster. If it travels that far in a second, imagine how far it could travel in an hour — 3600 times as far. Now try to visualise how far it could travel in an entire day, let alone a whole year.

Light can reach the Moon in just over a second. At that speed, the Sun is 8 light minutes from Earth, while Jupiter is on average about 20 light minutes distant. It takes four hours travelling at the speed of light to cross the orbit of Neptune, and to get to the nearest star we would have to travel for four and a half *years*. To travel right across the Milky Way galaxy, we would need nearly 100,000 years. Even at light speed it takes two and half million years to reach the Andromeda Galaxy. For light to travel from the remotest galaxies discovered at the edge of the observable universe, it requires about 10 billion Earth years!

SIZE AND PSYCHOLOGICAL IMPRESSIONS

Sizes can be deceiving. Test yourself and your friends with these questions.

A. How large do you think the Full Moon is when it is rising? Compare it to one of the following held at arm's length. Is it the size of:

1. a dinner plate? **2.** a saucer? **3.** a tennis ball? **4.** a 20 cent coin? **5.** your fingertip? **6.** a pea? or **7.** a pinhead?

B. How much larger is the Moon when it rises than when it is high in the sky? What do you think causes this phenomenon?

C. Which appears the larger in the sky, the Moon or the Sun? By how much and why?

The answers to these questions may surprise you.

ANSWERS

A. The Full Moon is easily covered by a pea or your little fingernail held at arm's length.

B. The Moon may look much larger when it is rising but it is an illusion. Because it is so bright and full of detail, psychologically, it can appear much larger than a featureless, dull pea which everyone knows is small. The Moon can also appear larger when it is rising because it can be related (subconsciously albeit) to distant earthly objects such as trees, buildings, ships or mountains that are known to be large but can be dwarfed by the Moon. It seems smaller when it is high above us because it is engulfed by a huge area of dark sky that makes it appear much smaller.

C. It is an amazing coincidence that the Sun is almost the same angular size as the Moon. To some people the brightness of the Sun can make it appear larger than the Moon.

The Moon often appears much larger when it is rising because it is easily compared to terrestrial objects. Photo: F Kohlhauf

CHAPTER THREE

TIPS ON PREPARING TO EXPLORE THE UNIVERSE

Observational astronomy may, at first, appear complex and technical, as if it requires a high level of skill, but this is an illusion that will quickly vanish if you apply some of the basic knowledge about observing contained in this chapter.

Naked-eye Observing: When observing with the naked eye or with small binoculars, it is often best to lie on a banana lounge or an airbed on the ground to eliminate straining your neck and back muscles and getting headaches. This is an easy way to observe meteor showers, satellites and to scan the Milky Way.

There is so much to see out there that naked-eye astronomy can occupy you for a considerable time. At some stage, however, you will probably want to see what an optical aid can do, so following are the basics of the equipment you can use.

Binoculars and Small Telescopes: As with many other hobbies or endeavours, it is usually best to start small and cautiously work your way up to large telescopes, if that is your ultimate desire. Even 7 x 50 binoculars will reveal so much that it is worth using them for a year or two before considering a telescope.

When buying binoculars, look through them to see how clear they are from the centre to the edge of the field of view. Good brands should be sharp well beyond halfway from the centre to the edge of the field of view. Binocular lenses that are tinted purplish-blue are the best because they allow most of the starlight to pass through the lenses into your eye.

Most common pairs of binoculars magnify 7 to 10 times. Large astronomical binoculars magnify 10 to 25 times but these are heavy and difficult to hold still, thereby requiring a mount.

Buying a Dream or a Nightmare? It is wise not to buy cheap department store telescopes because they are typically very unstable and

…e comets hit the Sun while others may become Sungrazers like Ikeya-Seki in 1965.
…ecame so bright it could be seen in daylight! This photograph, shot in the early
…rning from the centre of Perth, was taken with a simple camera using a short
…e exposure. Photo J Tompkins

This naked-eye view of the Milky Way through Centaurus, Crux and Carina extends from east of Alpha Centauri (brightest star at left) to the red Eta Carina Nebula (at right). The Southern Cross and the dark Coalsack Nebula adjoining it are at centre. Photo A Fujii

This extraordinarily beautiful region is the winter constellation Scorpius. The bright orange star Antares is enveloped in its own dust haze. The Lagoon Nebula is the pink object at lower right while the star clusters M7 and M6 are below the Scorpion's Sting top right. Note the dust lanes and the galactic centre (right). Photo A Fujii

often produce images that are dark, blurry and fringed with annoying chromatic colour caused by poor optics. Buy a reputable brand from a specialist telescope dealer or a second-hand telescope that you have already tested before purchasing. If uncertain, ask the opinion of an amateur astronomer in a local astronomy club, which will usually be listed in the phone book.

Aperture — Is Bigger Better? Aperture is a term that refers to the diameter of the telescope's objective lens (the large one at the front) if it is a refracting telescope, or the diameter of the main (largest) mirror of a reflecting telescope. The larger the aperture, the brighter the image and, if it is well made and collimated, the sharper the image. Knowing this, it is common to catch 'aperture fever' for, as they say, 'there's no substitute for aperture'. The problem is that, if you (or your friends) are not competent at making large telescopes, then they can be very costly to purchase, difficult to mount well, and cumbersome to transport.

Large apertures with short focal lengths around f4 to f6 can produce imperfect images if the optics are not carefully figured and collimated. Longer focal lengths of f8 to f15 are much more likely to produce sharper images and require less accurate collimation of the optics but they can be annoyingly long, requiring a ladder to reach the eyepiece.

Magnification: Don't be fooled by a telescope's magnifying power. Even fairly small telescopes can magnify nearly as much as large telescopes. My first telescope had a 60mm aperture and only one power, 30x, yet I was impressed as a boy to see the rings of Saturn, Jupiter's Moons, mountains and craters on the Moon as well as numerous star clusters and nebulae with it.

Small telescopes usually magnify from 30 to 300 times and large amateur telescopes typically have a range from 80 to 800, but sky conditions are seldom good enough to magnify more than 400 times. Because atmospheric turbulence affects large telescopes more so than small apertures, large telescopes cannot use very high powers all that often. More important than the size of the image is the clarity and the brightness of the image. A good beginner's telescope is a 60mm to 75mm refractor or a 100mm reflector. Most telescopes usually come with poor-quality eyepieces, making the purchase of good ones necessary to have the telescope perform at its best.

Small aperture telescopes are generally considered to be in the range of 60mm to 100mm. Moderate sizes are 150mm to 250mm, while large scopes have apertures of 300mm to 500mm. Anything larger is considered *very* large and only a dream for most. However, continuous improvements in telescope-making techniques, designs, technologies and materials are constantly reducing the cost, the weight and the bulkiness of large apertures and helping to make the optics better. Dobsonian telescope designs utilising large thin mirrors and simple, inexpensive mounts, allow even 46cm apertures to be made for a small fraction of the cost that a traditional design would cost. What would once have been a monstrous, heavy, permanent telescope, is now portable. In the not too distant future — with the aid of CCD electronics and computer enhancement — amateurs will be able to see more in their scopes than the 200 inch telescope could photograph a couple of decades ago. Amateur colour photography is beginning to surpass that already.

Eyepieces: There are many eyepiece brands on the market but the most impressive by far are Naglers and Meade's Ultrawide Field eyepieces. Both brands have such wide apparent fields of view (over 80°) that you think you are looking through a spaceship window rather than into an eyepiece. They are large and much more expensive than traditional eyepieces but worth every cent. They provide higher magnification while retaining a wide field.

Astronomy Clubs: It can be invaluable to attend some star parties organised by local astronomy clubs to get first-hand experience about observing and the various designs and brands of telescopes before purchasing one or building your own. You will meet people who will gladly assist you in building a telescope. Clubs can help you learn about many aspects of astronomy and you will have access to many astronomy books, magazines, videos and computer programs. Most capital cities have several clubs as do many large towns.

This inexpensive, practical and portable observatory was erected from several tarpaulins. It provides welcomed protection from wind and stray light.
Photo: GD Thompson

Comfort: Only when you are comfortable can you observe for long periods. Beginners can underestimate how cold it can get in winter standing relatively still for long periods at the eyepiece. Wear adequate clothing. Flying suits or showerproof and windproof, skisuit-like garments that zip over ordinary clothes are excellent. Used together with warm underwear, headwear, gloves, socks and fur-lined leather flying boots, they will keep you warm and comfortable. Be sure to wear clothing that does not let the wind penetrate.

An adequate supply of snacks and warm beverages is a must if you are planning a long observing session, as they will help keep you awake and warm. It is best not to drink alcohol or smoke as both detrimentally affect your night vision. Alcohol will also cause your body temperature to drop after a while and make you cold.

Protection from Wind: Exposure to wind can make you very cold and cause your telescope to vibrate, so set up behind an existing windbreak or make your own with tarpaulins supported by tent poles and ropes.

Using Large Binoculars: There are many sights in the heavens that only good binoculars show best. For instance, no telescope can show large bright comets, lunar eclipses, the Hyades and Pleiades star clusters, the Magellanic Clouds or large areas of the Milky Way as beautifully as binoculars do. Due to their higher magnifications, telescopes typically show too small a field of view for such objects.

Large binoculars need to be mounted. Unmounted, they will jump around too much to permit detail to be seen and they will become too heavy to hold for very long.

A traditional tripod mount will mean bending awkwardly to look at objects high in the sky. One way to overcome this problem is to place a large adjustable, good-quality flat mirror below the binoculars so that the binoculars can look *down* into the mirror to see the stars at a comfortable angle.

A binocular chair is an excellent mount for binoculars. A chair can be easily constructed using a second-hand car seat with an adjustable back and welding this to an old car wheel bearing assembly for azimuth (sideways) movement. Movement in the altitude (up and down) axis is achieved by a counterweighted, moving arm that holds the binoculars. This arm is supported by a lightweight frame which is attached to the seat back. So that the binoculars remain close to the eye when viewing at all altitudes, the altitude axis should pass through the point at which the neck pivots the head. To allow the binoculars to move out of the way when getting in and out of the chair, the binoculars can slide up or down a shaft that points skywards. Side tables and swinging tabletops can be added for holding star charts, torches, pens and so on.

Focusing Binoculars: To achieve the clearest and most relaxed view through binoculars, move the eyepieces closer together or further apart until they sit

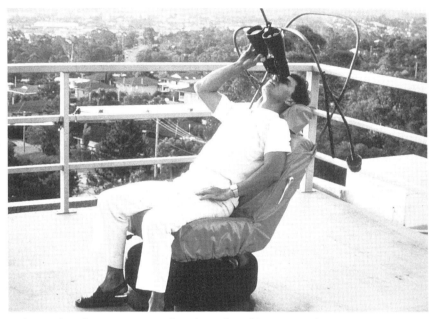

A binocular chair is a practical and comfortable means of supporting large binoculars. Photo: GD Thompson

comfortably in your eye sockets, allowing you to look straight into them and see no double images. (If you do see double images the binoculars may be out of collimation and need to be adjusted by an optical dealer or an optometrist.) The large focusing knob on the central rod between both eye-pieces provides a change of focus from near to far for both eyepieces. Relax your eyes and focus with the main focusing knob. Because many people have a different focus for each eye, most binoculars have a separate focusing capability for each eye. A secondary focusing mechanism, marked with a scale, is usually provided on the right eyepiece. To get perfect focus for both eyes, ignore your left eye so as to concentrate on the right eye focus. Turn the right eyepiece focusing knob until the image is crisp. Now open both eyes and make any final adjustments to both focusing knobs. Focus for a relaxed eye to eliminate eyestrain.

Telescopic Observing: To have a telescope perform well, you will need:
1. A stable telescope mount to eliminate it magnifying the slightest vibra-tions. (A solid mount will not be any value, however, if it is placed on a springy suspended timber verandah that bounces like a trampoline every time you breathe.)
2. Good collimation of the optics is necessary otherwise the telescope will lose light or have flares and blurry images, especially at higher powers. Reflector telescopes use concave and flat mirrors which are prone to mis-alignment, but refractors use lenses which are much less affected. If the

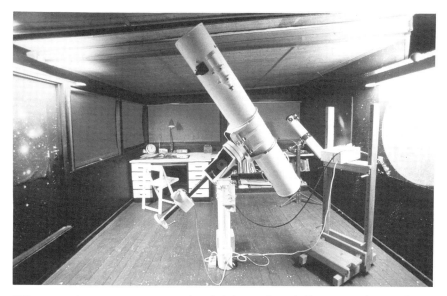

When my observatory was completed, it housed a solidly mounted 20cm f8 Newtonian reflector utilising large 20cm bearings. The aluminium mount is strong but lightweight. The German Equatorial mount was cleverly designed and constructed by expert amateur telescope-maker Cliff Duncan so that it disassembled into four manageable sections and three legs. It can be assembled in only a few minutes. Photo: GD Thompson

optics become dirty, contrast is lost so always store the telescope with its optical surfaces facing *downwards* whether dust caps are used or not. Dust never settles upwards.

3. A steady, non-turbulent atmosphere is especially necessary for observing fine astronomical detail. Often the atmosphere has at least three layers of air which can be moving in different directions and at different speeds. Where these layers interact, turbulence occurs. When we look at stars through such turbulence, it is like looking through the air turbulence in the heat above a fire. The image blurs and jumps around. When the atmosphere is steady through all its layers, astronomers call this *good seeing*.

4. Observational experience is invaluable. We all start out as novices. I remember my first views of Jupiter. All I saw were two faint brown bands across the temperate zones. Two years later after some dedicated observing, the same small telescope showed a wealth of detail: cyclones, streamers, eclipses, colours. This is common. Why? Because, with experience we learn how to get the perfect focus, how to recognise the best seeing conditions, to know when the planet is at its best, how to keep the object in the centre of the field of view where the image is the sharpest and so on. Experience especially teaches us to know what to look for and how to be patient enough to scrutinise tiny bits of detail instead of just quickly glancing at the whole view as beginners tend to do.

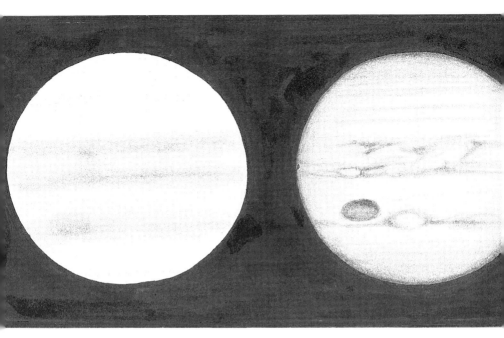

Inexperienced observers usually take short glances, not knowing what to look for and seeing little (left), whereas experienced observers will patiently scrutinise the image, enabling them to see the detailed view (right) in the same telescope. Drawings: GD Thompson

Sketching the Sky: I know of no way of gaining observational experience more quickly than drawing what you see. You do not need artistic skills to make this work for you. Sketching forces you to study the object in much more detail than you would otherwise do in order to draw it accurately.

You can start by making naked-eye drawings of the Moon or the changing positions of the planets as they move through the stars. Sketches made with mounted binoculars of deep sky objects or comets is a good learning experience.

Drawing really shows its advantages when recording telescopic observations. Even under the best seeing, it is impossible to have the air so steady that the whole image is perfectly sharp across the whole field. Drawing allows fine detail to be drawn as it appears. An extraordinarily detailed picture can be built up bit by bit. Serious drawings provide a lasting record of the observation that our memories cannot match. My detailed drawings of planets and deep sky objects reproduced in this book are drawn at the eyepiece and took 10 to 30 minutes each to make.

Use smooth-surfaced paper such as white photocopy paper; not textured paper that will cause rough spots on your drawing. A 2B pencil (with a good clean eraser) is the best for drawing pinpoint stars, and a blunt 4B pencil is excellent for smudging in diffuse objects.

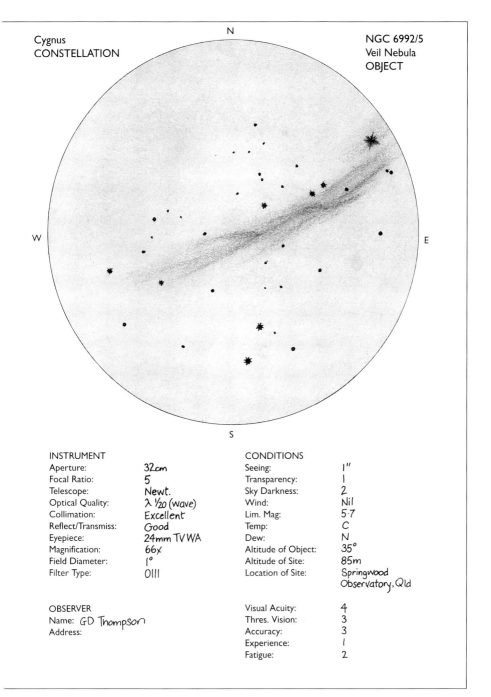

INSTRUMENT		CONDITIONS	
Aperture:	32cm	Seeing:	1″
Focal Ratio:	5	Transparency:	1
Telescope:	Newt.	Sky Darkness:	2
Optical Quality:	λ 1/20 (wave)	Wind:	Nil
Collimation:	Excellent	Lim. Mag:	5·7
Reflect/Transmiss:	Good	Temp:	C
Eyepiece:	24mm TV WA	Dew:	N
Magnification:	66x	Altitude of Object:	35°
Field Diameter:	1°	Altitude of Site:	85m
Filter Type:	OIII	Location of Site:	Springwood Observatory, Qld

OBSERVER			
Name:	GD Thompson	Visual Acuity:	4
Address:		Thres. Vision:	3
		Accuracy:	3
		Experience:	1
		Fatigue:	2

A drawing form such as this records all variable factors that can affect the observation, including those to do with the weather conditions, the telescope and the observer. Use a photocopy of the blank drawing form on page 127 to make your own drawings. Using the checklist on page 24, make note of the variable factors involved so that your drawing can be compared with other observer's drawings or your own in years to come.

OBSERVER'S CHECKLIST FOR MAKING DRAWINGS AND DESCRIPTIVE NOTES

Telescope Type Abbrev. as: N = Newtonian, C = Cassegrain, SC = Schmidt Cassegrain, D = Dobsonian, R = Refractor, B= Binoculars.

Optical Quality Express as a fraction of a wavelength of light.

Collimation Abbrev. as: E = Excellent, F = Fair, P = Poor.

Transmission Abbrev. as: G = Good, F = Fair, P = Poor.

Seeing Express in seconds of arc by testing close double stars.

Transparency Abbrev. as E = Excellent, G = Good, F = Fair, P = Poor, B = very bad

Sky Darkness 1 = Perfect, 2 = Fairly dark, 3 = 3-4 day moon, 4 = 7 day moon, 5 = full moon.

Wind Abbrev. as W = windy, S = Slight, N = Nil.

Temperature Abbrev. as F = Freezing, C = Cold, M = Mild, W= Warm, H = Hot.

Dew Abbrev. as H = Heavy, M = Mild, N = Nil.

Experience Abbrev. as 1 = Expert, 2 = Experienced, 3 = Casual observer, 4 = A little observing, 5 = Novice.

Fatigue 1 = Fresh, 2 = Little weary, 3 = Very tired

Accuracy 1 = Photographic, 2 = Object accurate, field fair, 3 = Object only fairly accurate, 4 = fairly rough, 5 = very rough, no detail

Description — For deep sky objects, note if:
(a) Visible to the naked eye or on view-finder.
(b) Surface Brightness — HSB = High eg. M42, Tuc 47, M17, NGC7009, M2.MSB = Medium eg. M57, M8, M87, M27, NGC253 LBS = Low, eg. M33, M101, Veil, Rosette, Helix, California, M74.
(c) Shape
(d) Diameter
(e) Dark Lanes
(f) Peculiar Features
(g) Surrounding Star Field

Galaxies Appearance of nucleus eg. starlike, broad core. Dark lanes. H II regions. Starcloud.

Star Clusters

Open Clusters Resolvability. Colours of Stars. Degree of concentration. Star Magnitudes.

C = Loose and irregular
D = Loose but roundish
E = Moderately concentrated
F = Fairly compressed
G = Very rich, compact

Globular Clusters

1 = Very open, poorly populated
3 = Sparse, slightly condensed
5 = Fairly populated but no nucleus
8 = Rich, condensed toward centre
10 = Very rich, very compressed.

Standard abbreviations – B = Bright(est), Bm = Brighter middle, DkLn = Dark Lane, El = Elongated, Irr = Irregular, M = Mottled, MW = Magnifies well, Nuc = Nucleus, PR = Partially resolved, R = Round, Sl = Slightly, * = Star, *like = Starlike, U = Unresolved, Vis = Visible, VF = Viewfinder, ! = Remarkable object.

High Magnification: High magnification generally provides maximum resolution. High power can be most effective on even very faint nebulous objects because it has the effect of darkening the background more than the object, thereby increasing contrast and making a difficult object more obvious. Small faint objects below the visibility threshold at low power can become large enough at higher powers to turn on the minimum number of rod cells in the eye to make the object visible. Be sure not to magnify more than the seeing conditions can stand though, otherwise you will make a blurry image a bigger blur.

Throughout the book, reference is made to low, medium and high power. For our purposes they shall mean magnifications between the following ranges:

Very Low Power = 30x to 60x
Low Power = 60x to 120x
Medium Power = 120x to 250x
High Power = 250x to 400x
Very High Power = 400x to 800x

Filters: Used properly, some filters can be of enormous assistance in making the invisible, visible. Coloured filters can have some minor advantage in bringing out details on Mars and to some extent on Jupiter. Martian frosts are a little more obvious with a blue filter, and duststorms are more obvious with a yellow filter.

Moon filters are simply used to reduce the glare of the Moon when viewed through a telescope. They can stop you from walking around half blinded from a dark spot in your eye caused by the intensity of the Moon's image.

Glass Sun filters that go over the eyepiece of small telescopes provide great resolution but at a high price — your eyesight! They almost always crack from the Sun's heat.

Aluminised Mylar solar filters that go over the front end of the telescope are the safest way to observe the Sun by reflecting 99.99% of the Sun's light. They do not seem to deliver the full resolution capabilities of the telescope's aperture, and they tint the Sun a bluish colour.

Hydrogen alpha solar filters are marvellous because they permit the Sun's prominences to become visible, but they can cost hundreds or thousands of dollars depending on the brand and type.

Deep sky filters produce the most impressive results because they effectively cut out unwanted artificial and natural background light in order to greatly increase the contrast of emission nebulae. The *Ultra High Contrast* filter and the *Oxygen III* filter do a superb job. Essentially, they only let through the visible green light emitted from emission nebulae. The OIII filter only transmits the light of doubly ionised oxygen, which is abundant in most nebulae. Both filters stop nearly all urban sky glow as well as moonlight and even airglow. Not only do they do wonders in the city but they even enhance dark sky viewing by making the background sky virtually pitch-black. They are expensive but are worth it because, in effect, they make your telescope perform as if it had greater aperture.

There is a *Hydrogen Beta* deep sky filter but I have only seen it significantly enhance the Horsehead Nebula. Unfortunately, there is no effective filter to enhance stars or galaxies. Most astronomy magazines such as *Sky & Space* (Australia), *Sky & Telescope* (USA) or *Astronomy* (USA), frequently advertise such accessories and suppliers.

Telescope Observing Chair: For comfortable telescopic viewing, an adjustable height chair and table is a must. If the telescope eyepiece changes height when moving from one object to another then so should the chair and table. The larger the telescope, the more likely it is that you will need to make a specially designed chair and/or footstool with a swinging benchtop that has many variations in height.

Computer-aided Telescopes: The traditional means of finding objects in the sky has been to locate the object on a star atlas and then star-hop from bright naked-eye stars to fainter telescopic ones, using the telescope's viewfinder, until the object is located. The process usually takes 5 to 15 minutes depending on the difficulty of the object. To overcome this, computerised devices can be fitted to telescopes that allow the observer to zero in exactly onto a preselected object within seconds by simply moving the telescope until all zeros show on a light-emitting diode (LED) display.

CHAPTER FOUR

MAKING THE MOST OF YOUR EYES

To become a good observer, one needs to learn how to observe. That means learning how to use one's eyes to best advantage under faint light and how to observe for long enough to see what is really there.

Dark Adaption: When we walk from a bright glary environment into the dark, we are temporally blinded until our eyes adapt to the darkness. At least a few minutes are needed for a healthy eye to become dark adapted enough to see faint stars.

If you are keen on searching for very faint objects, it can help if you wear dark sunglasses during the afternoon prior to observing. This will increase your eye's sensitivity to faint light. To achieve maximum sensitivity to faint light at the telescope, use a dark cloth over your head when looking into the

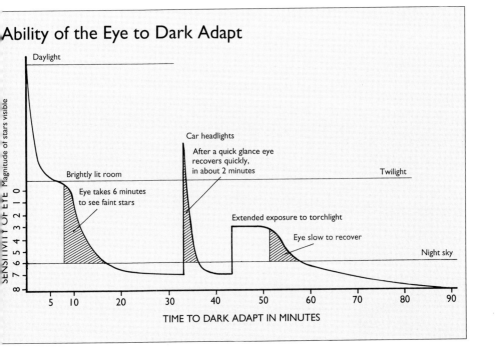

Ability of the Eye to Dark Adapt

eyepiece. This stops stray light from entering your eyes from the sides and it considerably improves your dark adaption. As the graph shows, the dark adapted eye will recover more quickly to a *short* exposure to very bright light than to a longer exposure of dull light, so keep your torchlight as dim as possible.

Averted Vision: Mastering the use of averted vision will allow you to see faint objects that would otherwise be invisible. It comes into play when we do not look directly at something, but rather, out of the corner of our eye. We 'avert' our vision to see very faint light because our eye's cone cells at the centre of vision are only good for seeing fine detail and colour, whereas the more outlying rod cells beyond 20° off centre are the most sensitive to faint light. Test this by observing some faint naked-eye star clusters and nebulae and you will notice how averted vision makes them much more obvious when you do not look directly at them. It works best when you move your centre of vision around every half second or so while keeping your concentration fixed on the area of interest.

Perseverance: Whether you are observing with the naked eye or using a large amateur telescope, be assured that perseverance will let you see things and make discoveries that you might otherwise think are impossible. Sometimes it just takes dedication and lots of time to observe the unusual, such as the moons of Uranus, the changing seasons on Mars, or to discover a new comet or supernova.

Torchlight: To see in the dark you will need some light. When your eyes are dark adapted, the faintest light seems so bright! So that your torchlight does not blind you every time you illuminate your star atlas, cover the torch with red cellophane or brown paper to dull its light. This will help maintain the sensitivity of your eyes. Use enough paper to give a soft dull glow just bright enough to read your star charts. Some torches will need black tape around the sides to stop side light from entering your eyes. If power is handy, a children's night light at the end of a power lead is a fine light source that doesn't need batteries.

Stray Light: If you are looking at anything but very bright objects — such as the Moon or the bright planets — then you will find stray light annoying. Even a low wattage fluorescent light half a kilometre away can send you ballistic when you are observing at the threshold of vision, looking for that faint comet or galaxy. Working from inside a comfortable observatory can solve this but out in the open you will need that dark cloth over the head.

Aging Eyes: As we age our eyes deteriorate. Because the eye does not replace old cells but, rather, grows new cells on the older ones, the old cells are retained and the lens becomes clouded, reducing the transmission of faint light. With age, it yellows. This tends to filter out blue light. After 50 years of age, blues seem progressively duller and by mid-60s, deep violet light can become invisible. Furthermore, the iris — the coloured streaky area surrounding the black pupil — begins to shrink also. The iris permits the pupil to dilate by opening and closing like a camera aperture diaphragm. This controls the amount of light entering the eye so we are not blinded by too much, or too little light. When we are young, it opens the pupil to 7mm or 8mm in diameter in the dark to let in maximum light, but when we are 50 it can often be only 5mm wide, causing very faint objects to become invisible.

Another consequence of aging is that as our eye lens solidifies, we lose our ability to be able to focus on very close objects. It becomes increasingly difficult to change focus from a star chart 30cm away to the stars at infinity. If you wear glasses for long or short sightedness, they do not have to be used when looking through binoculars or telescopes. The instrument's focusing mechanism will bring the object into clear focus with, or without, your glasses. Not using your glasses will give you a larger field of view in the telescope because your eye can get closer.

When looking at bright stars or the Moon against a dark sky, aging will increase the likelihood of noticing double vision, spikes and flares caused from ripples and imperfections in the clear cornea that covers the surface of the eye. Generally, such astigmatism can be overcome by correctly prescribed glasses.

HOW DARK IS THE NIGHT?

A naturally dark night sky is not pitch-black, as people often assume. On a moonless night at a dark sky site, place your hand or a dark object against the sky and note how much brighter the sky is. You will notice that the trees are truly black but the atmosphere is a much lighter, dark bluish colour. In a naturally dark sky, the clouds should always be dark. If they are brighter than the sky, it is because they're lit from below by artificial light.

The reason the sky is not jet black is due to *airglow*. Air molecules in the upper atmosphere glow from being bombarded by cosmic rays from space. Furthermore, just as sunlight and moonlight brighten the sky, so does starlight. If we had no atmosphere to glow then the night sky would be truly black, just like it is on the Moon. We would be able to see stars to magnitude 8.5!

CHAPTER FIVE

OBSERVING THE SUN, THE EARTH AND THE MOON IN MOTION

As the Moon orbits the Earth and, in turn, the Earth orbits the Sun we are constantly seeing both the Sun and the Moon from different angles and distances. This produces many interesting phenomena, some of which we will explore in this chapter.

THE SUN AND THE EARTH

The Travelling Sun: Watch the Sun set every afternoon and you will notice that it sets in a slightly different spot. The tilt of the Earth's axis and the Earth's motion around the Sun make the Sun change its setting position by approximately its apparent diameter each day. It is interesting to photograph sunset over a distant horizon from the same location regularly from the *Winter Solstice* on 22 June, the shortest day of the year, to the *Summer Solstice* on 22 December, the longest day of the year, to see how far it moves over that time.

Watching the Earth Rotate: It is surprising how few people have ever watched the Sun set even though it only takes approximately two minutes from when the Sun first touches the horizon until it completely disappears. When they watch the Sun set, most people are surprised that they can actually watch the Earth rotate.

If you have a very low horizon and clear air, you may see a phenomenon called the *Green Flash*, where the last bead of the Sun actually turns lime to emerald green: that is, if you are lucky enough to get the right atmospheric conditions. It is much more obvious in binoculars or telescopes. The Sun is much less bright near a low horizon because the thickness of the atmosphere at such a low altitude will absorb the Sun's harmful rays and most of its light, often making it possible to observe it with the naked eye. It is a good rule to never stare at the Sun, even at very low altitudes, if it is bright enough to cause discomfort.

Earth's Shadow in the Sky: After the Sun has set, the Earth's shadow passes through our atmosphere and it slowly becomes visible every clear evening in the low eastern sky. You will need a low distant horizon to see it well. The shadow appears as a grey, arching feature opposite the Sun that tapers off to the northeast and southeast. The curving shape of the shadow testifies to the Earth being round. The shadow will rise as the Sun sets, gradually becoming less distinct until the whole sky is dark.

The Mysterious Zodiacal Light: In a dark site, it is fascinating to look into the western sky at the end of twilight, or the eastern sky before morning twilight, and observe sunlight reflecting off interplanetary dust particles. The light extends along the Zodiac and hence it is called the *Zodiacal Light*. Although it is actually fainter than the Milky Way, it can appear so bright that you could be mistaken for thinking it is the sky glow from a large city just over the horizon. It appears like a half spindle of light 10° wide rising out of the horizon from where the Sun sets or rises. Many people in the country see it but incorrectly assume it is the Sun's afterglow or twilight in the Earth's atmosphere when it is actually light from far out in space.

The elusive Zodiacal Light photographed from Siding Spring Observatory after evening twilight. Photo: GD Thompson

It usually fades out about 40° to 60° degrees away from the Sun, but a very dark, transparent sky will allow it to be visible right across the sky. At a point directly opposite the Sun along the Zodiacal Light, there is a slight increase in its breath and brightness. This challenging phenomena is called the *Counter Glow*. It is an oval of very faint light 15° x 20°. To see the Zodiacal Light and especially the Counter Glow, be sure that the Milky Way is not near its position, otherwise there will not be enough contrast to make it visible.

Observing Storms on the Sun: If you look carefully with your naked eye at the Sun's disc when it is very close to the horizon, you will sometimes detect black spots on it. If the Sun is high in the sky, use a piece of welding glass to protect your eyes. These spots are magnetic storms called *Sunspots*, which are cooler than the Sun's surrounding surface. When the Sun's light is

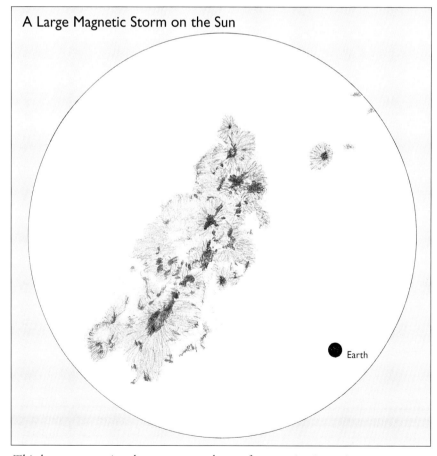

A Large Magnetic Storm on the Sun

Earth

This large magnetic solar storm was drawn from projection using a 32cm telescope. The dot indicates the comparative size of the Earth.
Drawing: GD Thompson

reduced so that it is comfortable to look at, Sunspots, which are actually white hot, appear black compared with the Sun's much hotter surrounding photosphere. If they are large enough to be seen with the naked eye, they arc many times larger than our planet!

A simple way to observe Sunspots is to project the image of the Sun through binoculars or a telescope onto white paper — they will appear clearly if present. When viewed with a telescope, you will see that they have a dark centre called the *umbra* surrounded by a grey, lacy-looking *penumbra*. If you draw them, you will notice that they change in shape from hour to hour or day to day depending on the magnification used.

Even naked-eye observation of large Sunspot groups over a few days will clearly reveal that they move across the Sun's face. This is due to the Sun's rotation once every 25 days at its equator, and 35 days at its poles. Because the Sun's equator is inclined to the Ecliptic just as Earth's axis is, Sunspots only travel straight across the Sun in December and June. At other times, they move in arcs because we are a little above or below the Sun's equator.

Sunspots tend to stay mostly within 30° of the Sun's equator. They are formed when the Sun's magnetic field lines come to the surface. They are usually formed in pairs; one being the opposite polarity to the other. Sunspots are typically 1000 to 10,000km below the rest of the Sun's turbulent surface, and this is obvious when they move close to the limb of the Sun as they have a crater-like appearance. The Edge of the Sun or Moon's disc is referred to as the limb. The Sunspot cycle comes to a peak about every 11 years and will do so again around the turn of this century.

Huge solar flares called *Prominences* can be ejected up to 1.5 million kilometres from the Sun's yellow surface, which is known as the *photosphere*. These can only be observed with hydrogen alpha filters or during a Total Eclipse of the Sun, when they are seen as fantastic, hot pink flames leaping from the Sun's limb in ultra slow-motion.

ORBITAL MOTION

Following the Moon in its Orbit around the Earth: From a calendar, find out when it will be New Moon. One or two nights later, look for its thin crescent during the twilight low in the western to northwestern sky. If you want to watch the Moon orbit the Earth, observe the Moon every night from New Moon on. You will see how it moves further and further away from the Sun as it moves along its orbit. At its furtherest point, it is Full Moon. The reverse then occurs as it moves into the early morning sky.

After New Moon, as it orbits the Earth, you will also notice that more of the Moon becomes illuminated. When it is a New Moon, we see mostly the dark side of the Moon because it is almost between us and the Sun.

At New Moon, the dark side can be seen faintly due to *Earthshine* lighting up the dark side far more intensely than the Full Moon lights up our night-time landscape. The bright reflective clouds of Full Earth reflect

Around New Moon, the dark side of the Moon is illuminated by Full Earthshine. Photo: T Dickinson

10 times as much sunlight as does the dark grey lunar soil. From the Moon, the Earth appears 6 times larger than the Moon does to us. So a Full Earth is 60 times as bright as a Full Moon.

Satellites: It is very easy to observe satellites in orbit around the Earth. In low Earth orbit, they travel right around Earth in only 90 minutes so their motion across the sky is most obvious, but they don't move nearly as fast as shooting stars. Their speed is more like the speed of a plane at moderate altitude. Satellites appear just like a moving star. If the satellite is large then it will appear bright, providing it is in sunlight.

Satellites are best seen in the evening just as the sky is darkening or in the morning before twilight begins. At these times, the satellite is high enough (160km, on average) to be catching sunlight, whereas the surface of the Earth below and the atmosphere above the observer is still in shadow or darkness. It is common when watching satellites moving away from the Sun to see them start to become redder and fade, because the Sun is setting on them as they move into the shadow of the Earth.

Sometimes satellites tumble and change in brightness due to different surfaces reflecting more or less sunlight. I remember watching Skylab pass overhead and seeing it rise dramatically in brightness to approximately magnitude -8 for a second or two. It looked as if it was exploding! The solar panel caught the Sun and caused a specular reflection just like a distant mirror reflecting the Sun. Only three orbits before it burnt up over Esperence in Western Australia, I also saw it give another brilliant specular reflection while it was only 4.5° over the southern horizon as it passed 120km above Sydney!

ECLIPSES

A Darkening Sun: As the Moon moves around its orbit it regularly passes in front of a portion of the Sun causing a *Partial Solar Eclipse*. If the Moon totally covers the Sun, it is called a *Total Solar Eclipse*. These are rare and occur only along a narrow corridor across the Earth's surface. Anyone who has been fortunate enough to witness this natural spectacle will attest to the value of travelling across the world to see it. These occur about every year or two but are not always favourably placed. As the Sun is stationary, a solar eclipse is an easy way to watch the Moon moving along in space. A partial solar eclipse is best observed by projecting the image of the Sun through binoculars or a telescope onto a large white card placed in a dark room, if possible.

Bronze Moonshine: On average, about a couple of times a year the Moon will travel into the Earth's shadow and a *Lunar Eclipse* occurs. When the Moon is partially eclipsed, the eclipsed portion will usually go a beautiful orange-bronze colour if the Earth's atmosphere contains appreciable dust and smoke to redden the Sun's light as it passes through the atmosphere on its way to the Moon. If the Moon travels near the centre of the Earth's shadow, it can become so dark grey it can disappear. Because a totally eclipsed Moon is much less bright than when it was a fully illuminated Full Moon, faint stars will become visible and an ethereal atmosphere is likely to engulf you — especially if you are observing away from city lights with a glass of good red and appropriate music to suit the event! As you watch this spectacle, you will witness further proof of the Earth being round, revealed by the shape of its shadow. The motion of the Moon around the Earth will also be apparent as it moves through the Earth's shadow over a few hours.

THE MAGNIFICENT MOON

The Moon is a most striking and memorable sight for most people looking into a telescope for the first time. It is extremely bright and has stark contrast. There is so much that can be said about this fascinating but lifeless world that numerous books have been written on it alone. To do the Moon justice, you will need to acquire a good lunar atlas detailing all its features.

The Best Time to Observe Lunar Detail: The Moon has numerous features scattered all over it but the time to see some of the best is a couple of days either side of Half Moon — usually called *First Quarter*. (This is about 7 days after New Moon, when the Moon is a quarter of the way around its 28 day orbit.) *Last Quarter* (seven days after Full Moon) is just as good, but you have to get up early in the morning to see it. At First Quarter, the *terminator* forms a nearly straight line between the cusps or tips of the Moon. The terminator is where the day side meets the night side, that is, where sunrise or sunset occurs on the Moon. The Sun is very low in the sky on the Moon along the terminator, causing long shadows to be cast which define the lunar terrain well. At Full Moon, the Sun is high in the sky over most of the Moon and there are virtually no shadows to show relief, only differences in the reflectivity of the lunar soil. Crater ejecta rays can be best seen at this time.

Lunar Rock 'n' Roll: Although the Moon keeps the same face towards us, we, in fact, see not 50% of it, but almost 60%. This *Libration* effect is caused by the tilt of the Moon's orbit, the orbit's elliptical shape and the direction from which it is viewed from Earth. These factors combine to allow us to see 'around the sides' of the Moon. It appears to rock back and forth and up and down a little as it orbits the Earth. The viewing angle combinations caused by Libration together with the ever-changing Sun angles are so enormous that it would be virtually impossible to see any Lunar feature lit exactly the same, and viewed from the same angle, in a lifetime! So, every time you observe the Moon you are getting a different view.

Seas of Lava: A naked-eye view of the Moon shows dark markings that are often called the 'Man in the Moon', which were once thought to be lunar seas, hence they were named *Mare* (Latin for seas). Good binoculars and telescopes will show the Mare as large, relatively flat plains of dark lava that flowed out of the Moon's core about three billion years ago. It flooded the low-lying areas, some of which were basins (enormous craters) formed from very large asteroidal impacts in the Moon's first billion years when it was totally covered in craters. Smaller and fresher craters have impacted on the 'seas' since. Telescopic inspection of the Mare along the terminator will show subtle wave-like ridges caused by buckling of the lunar surface from internal geological forces.

Explosive Craters: Binoculars will depict the largest craters and a moderate-sized telescope will reveal incredible detail. On a steady night, you can sit for hours looking into a high-powered eyepiece, moving slowly along the Moon's terminator from one feature to the next, and repeat this night after night as the terminator moves. A good telescope will make you feel like you are flying over the terrain.

The majority of craters are in the highland regions that have not been flooded. One of the most impressive is the old, large *Clavius*. It measures 230km in diameter. Four smaller craters arc across its interior. The crater *Tycho* is prominent with obvious white ejecta rays that are particularly visible around Full Moon. Tycho is about 100km in diameter and has steep high walls.

The Appenine Mountain Range, at left, is the remains of the wall of an enormous crater formed after the impact of the meteorite that created Mare Imbrium early in the Moon's history. Hundreds of millions of years later, lava flooded the low-lying areas to form the plains — dark areas. Huygens Rile, above centre, appears as a fine white line.

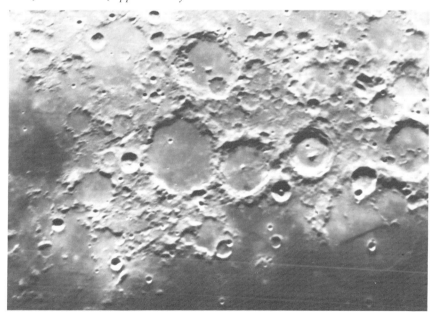

The large old crater Pontanus, near centre, has a flooded floor while more recent craters do not. The Straight Wall is at lower right. Photos: J Barclay

The energy released when an asteroid or meteor comes to a sudden halt by impacting with the Moon (or any other body) is enormous. The body that exploded the Tycho crater would have been only 6 to 10kms in diameter yet it released 2000 times as much energy as would be released if every atomic bomb ever made by every nation was simultaneously exploded. *Copernicus* is another stunning crater to observe a few days after First Quarter. It has terraced walls and a central mountain peak formed from molten rock in the centre that rebounded after the shock of the impact. Material ejected from the blast created secondary craters in the Mare when it splattered back across the surrounding surface.

Microscopic meteorites left over from the formation of the Solar System have been pulverising the surface of the Moon for billions of years, covering it in a talcum powder-like dust that the astronauts left their footprints in.

Lunar Mountain Ranges: The Moon is much less massive than Earth. It would take over 81 Moons to equal Earth's mass. Because the gravity is so much less, lunar mountains are taller than Earth's when compared in their respective diameters. As the Moon has no atmosphere, there is no wind or water erosion to erode the mountains away. The mountains on the Moon look rugged in the small telescope but they are, in fact, rather smooth and undulating. The most easily observed range is the *Apennines*, which encircle almost half of *Mare Imbrium*. Its highest peak, *Mt Huygens*, rises to 6000m. Further to the Moon's north, this range becomes the *Alps Mountains*.

The old, heavily cratered highland region around the large crater Clavius.
Photo: J Barclay

Lunar Rivers and Lava Tubes: Water never ran on the Moon, but lava did. The lava often flowed underground in lava tubes that are very similar to those around volcanoes on Earth, but much larger. On the Moon, they can be as long as hundreds of kilometres and up to 2km in diameter. If the roof collapses, they form river-like features such as *Schroter's Valley*, nicknamed the 'Cobra Head', near the brilliant white crater *Aristarchus*. Others are *Huygens Rile*, near the centre of the Moon, and the riles around the crater *Triesneckner*.

Domes and Clefts: Subtle dome-like rises in the Mare, called *Lunar Domes*, can often be detected along the terminator in larger instruments. They are thought to be formed from volcanic gas building up under overlying soil and lava to form a type of shallow bubble effect. Faults and fissures abound on the Moon. In small telescopes, look for the *Straight Wall*, which is a fine example of a *Lunar Fault*. It is an angled cliff 250m high and 130km long joining a high plain to a low plain. The *Alpine Valley* is an enormous valley 130km long and about 10km wide, 'cut' through the Alps when they were torn apart by movement of the Moon's crust. When the lowlands flooded with lava, so did the lower portion of the Alpine Valley.

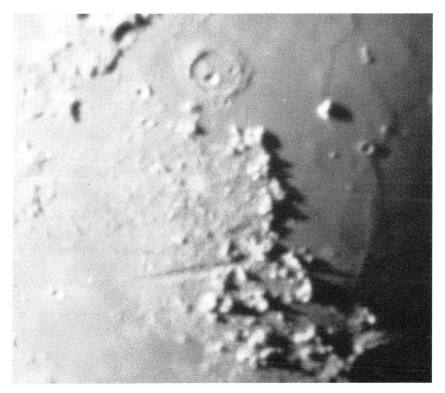

The Alpine Valley cuts right through the Alps mountain range. Photo: S Quirk

THE EVER-CHANGING PLANETS

A planet is a large body of solid and/or liquid matter that orbits a star or stars. It is the leftover debris from the formation of a star that is not massive enough to become a star itself. Some smaller 'planets' can orbit larger planets. Our Solar System has not just the nine main planets but over 30 major worlds (major and minor planets) that are constantly presenting their unique peculiarities to us in many different ways. Our telescopes can display these distant 'specks of dust' to us in surprising detail when we know what to look for.

The Size of the Solar System: To visualise the relative sizes of the planets and the distances between them in human terms, imagine shrinking the Sun to the size of a huge beach ball 70cm (30") across. At this scale, Earth would be orbiting some 75m away and be the size of a pea. Mercury, the nearest planet to the Sun, would be 30m from the beach ball but only be about the size of a pinhead. Giant Jupiter would be the size of a tennis ball and lie 400m away. Uranus would be the diameter of a 10 cent coin lying nearly 1.5 km away. Pluto would be a speck 3km down the road! At this scale, the nearest star would be an incredible two and a half times the diameter of our whole planet away!! As we can see, the Solar System and interstellar space consists of only minute specks of matter in vast volumes of space.

The Sun's family of planets orbit the Sun, not in circles but in ellipses or ovals, causing their distance from the Sun to change somewhat. It also means that their closest distance to Earth can change from one year to the next. For instance, Mars will not be at its very closest to us until 2003 and 2005, when it will appear 1.5 times larger than it does in the 1990s. The nearby planets, such as Mars and Venus, change much in apparent size as they move to and from us. As the outer planets are much further away, this effect is greatly reduced.

The Evening and Morning Stars: The two planets that orbit between the Earth and the Sun are Mercury and Venus. Because their orbits are small

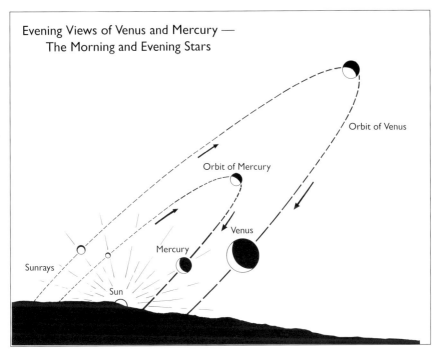

Evening Views of Venus and Mercury —
The Morning and Evening Stars

Venus and Mercury can be observed after sunset or before sunrise. As they travel along their orbits their apparent size changes. Only these inner planets show such dramatic phase effects.

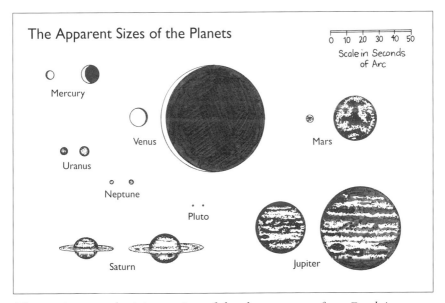

The Apparent Sizes of the Planets

The maximum and minimum sizes of the planets as seen from Earth in a telescope.

compared to the planets that orbit outside the Earth, Mercury and Venus never move very far from the Sun. They are seen only for a short time after dark or before morning twilight; never late at night. Both Mercury and Venus display phases like the Moon. When they are on the far side of the Sun they appear as small, fully illuminated discs, but when they are at their greatest elongation (separation) from the Sun they appear much larger with half of the planet illuminated and the other half in darkness, like a First Quarter Moon. As they continue to move closer to Earth in their orbits, they continue to grow much larger, and this can be observed from night to night in small telescopes. The illuminated portion of the planet shrinks to the shape of a crescent moon as it moves between us and the Sun. Neither Mercury nor Venus are likely to show markings.

Mercury: Mercury is the closest planet to the Sun, at a distance of 58 million kilometres. It is less than 5000km in diameter, being 2.5 times smaller than our planet and not much larger than the Moon. It is an airless Moon-like world that is totally saturated in craters with very little in the way of flat plains. Mercury is pretty much preserved as it was less than a billion years after the formation of the Solar System, 4.6 billion years ago. Mercury suffered a massive impact which caused the largest feature, the *Caloris Basin* — a circular remnant of mountains and fractures some 2000km across. The impact was so extreme that shock waves travelled right through the planet to the other side and created an area of chaotic hills 1.5km high covered in fractures. Mercury's dark soil reflects only one-tenth of the Sun's light.

Mercury only stays visible for a few weeks at a time during its short 88 day orbit around the Sun. It rotates three times every two orbits. Its day side temperature can reach 430°C, yet it drops to a cold 170°C on the night side.

Mercury appears as a yellowish-white star fairly low in the west when it is in the evening sky, or low in the east before dawn. It never moves any further than 28° from the Sun. It shines brightly at magnitude 0 to -1, but it appears fainter because it is always seen low in the sky through dense murky air or in twilight skies. Unfortunately, few people ever see Mercury because they don't have a low horizon. To make viewing more challenging still, Mercury is only easily visible for about 30 minutes once the sky starts to darken after twilight. Because Mercury revolves around the Sun so fast, it only remains well placed each apparition for a couple of weeks.

Venus: This planet is so intensely bright that it is often mistaken for a UFO. At magnitude -4, it far outshines all other stars and planets. Venus is similar in size to the Earth, but it has a carbon dioxide atmosphere and a 600°C surface temperature. The rocky surface is totally hidden under white clouds of sulphuric acid, which reflect most of the Sun's light and make it appear so brilliant. The sunlight that does get through the clouds is trapped, causing a greenhouse effect. The atmospheric density is an incredible 90 times that of Earth. The high atmospheric pressure and the torrid temperature

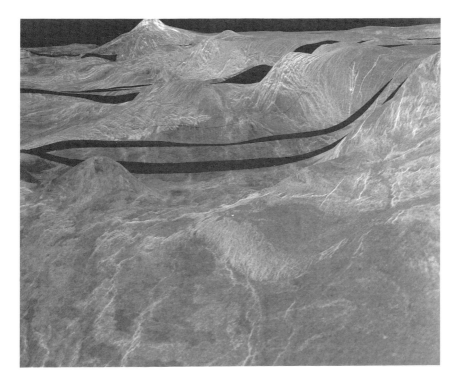

The Magellan space probe mapped Venus in astonishing detail. Computers have produced numerous remarkable pictures from the data received. This one shows the plateau Lakshmi Planum dropping precipitiously down to the lowlands near Ishtar Terra, a highland region the size of Australia. The volcano in the background is one of many. It rises 6km above the surface of the plateau. (The black lines are sections of missing coverage.) Photo: NASA

create a strange effect that causes flat, distant horizons to appear as if they are high in the sky, as if one were always in a crater. This refraction of light effect can be seen when one wears goggles in a swimming pool and looks upwards just under the surface. The sides of the pool look like they are overhead.

Incredibly, the atmosphere rotates 60 times faster than the planet. Venus is the only planet in the Solar System to rotate slowly backwards, possibly due to some major impact three or four billion years ago.

The Magellan space probe mapped a spectacular terrain of volcanoes, lava 'pancakes', crevasses, mountains, impact craters, ejecta blankets, sand-dunes, faults, fractures and numerous other geological features.

Venus is so bright it can easily be seen during the day at greatest elongation from the Sun. Daytime is actually the best time to view it in a telescope when it is high in the sky.

When it moves towards inferior conjunction (its closest approach to the Sun), it is interesting to follow it as close as possible to the Sun to see the crescent become ever so thin. With excellent conditions, perseverence and sensible precautions, Venus can be seen when it is near the Sun as a ring of light. Sunlight is refracted through Venus' atmosphere around the dark side and back to us.

The Red Planet: Mars is one of the finest planets to observe. It is best seen every couple of years as the Earth overtakes it in its orbit. Mars is called the red planet because its soil is very reddish, due to it being predominantly made up of iron oxides similar to rust. Earth is roughly twice as large as Mars. The atmosphere on Mars is very thin and composed of mainly carbon dioxide. Like Earth, Mars has polar icecaps, which are easily visible in small telescopes when it is winter, in the hemisphere that tilts towards us. The caps are made of mostly frozen carbon dioxide (dry ice). A small water icecap is all that remains during the summer.

Mars' dark markings can be seen in small telescopes. (They were once thought by some to be signs of a Martian civilisation that used canals for irrigation.) As the seasons change on Mars, wind blows dust and sand over, or away from, these purplish-brown areas, making their intensity and shape

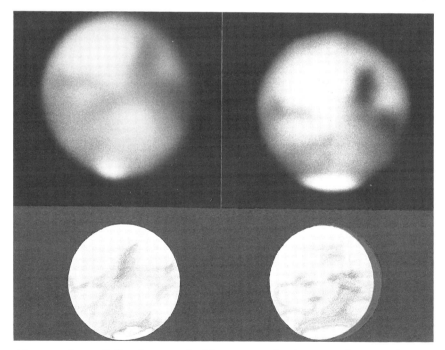

Mars was beautifully photographed by Barry Adcock using a homemade 32cm reflector. Note the difference in size of the icecap and the darkness of the prominent lung-shaped feature called Syritis Major. Left: Winter, July 1986. Right: Summer, 5 September 1988. The drawings below show different sides of the planet. Left: 20 July 1971, 20cm f6 400x. Right: 4 August 1971, 20cm 200x. Note the section of the icecap breaking away as it melts.
Drawings: GD Thompson

change to some degree. Careful observation will detect bluish-white morning frosts on the planet's limb or yellowish dust storms erupting. Martian winds can become so fierce that a dust storm can cover the whole planet in only a week or so, obliterating all surface markings.

Mars has several, apparently inactive, volcanoes. The highest one, *Mons Olympus* — the Olympic Mountain — is so high it reaches into outer space. It is three times as high as Mt Everest. The whole of Brisbane could fit into the caldera at its summit, and its base would stretch halfway from Brisbane to Sydney. Sometimes the long white clouds that form around it may be glimpsed in large amateur telescopes.

Another incredible martian feature is *Valles Marineris*. It is a gigantic version of the Grand Canyon, in Arizona, that is so long it could stretch across Australia. The deepest sections lie 7km below the surrounding plains.

Mars has two small asteroid-like moons, *Phobos* and *Deimos*, whose brightness would make them visible in amateur telescopes if they weren't lost in Mars' glare.

The Roving Asteroids: Between the orbits of Mars and Jupiter roam a myriad of asteroids or minor planets. *Ceres* is the largest at 1000km in diameter and there are 200 or so larger than 100km in diameter. The smaller they become, the more there are. Many, such as *Pallas*, the second largest at 600km in diameter, appear to be double; both components in orbit around one another as they orbit the Sun together. The smaller asteroids are, the more irregular they appear. *Vesta* is like a short cucumber, changing in brightness as it rotates. It can become bright enough to be faintly detected with a keen naked eye. *Juno*, Ceres and Pallas can be detected in binoculars when they are close to Earth. Astronomy magazines and Ephemerides give the positions of asteroids when they are at their brightest. In the telescope, they appear like a star moving very slowly past nearby stars over many hours or days.

More and more Earth-grazing asteroids are being discovered as they pass dangerously close to Earth. There are 10,000 estimated to exist that could impact with Earth at some future time. In 1906, a chunk of ice from Encke's Comet exploded as it struck the Earth's atmosphere over Siberia. Although it did not reach the surface, it flattened 100sq km of forest and the sonic boom was heard in London!

Incredible as it seems, an asteroid only 1km in diameter can release so much explosive energy when it impacts that it could do as much damage as a full-scale nuclear war. It would throw so much dust and smoke into the atmosphere that it would cause a 'nuclear winter' effect. Sunlight would be reduced enough to stop photosynthesis and kill plankton, thereby destroying the food chain and most lifeforms. Enormous earthquakes, tidal waves, fires and atmospheric shock waves would sweep around the world and Earth would lose some of its atmosphere.

After a few years or decades, weather would start to stabilise again and evolution would once again begin the process of evolving new species and regrowing old survivors. Our planet was once as saturated with impact

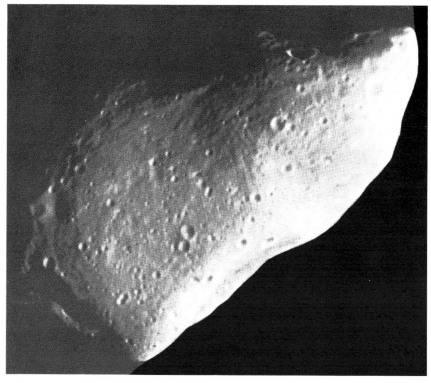

The Galileo space probe en route to Jupiter took this first-ever photograph of an asteroid in the Asteroid Belt. Gaspra is heavily cratered, very irregular and measures only 20 x 12 x 11km. Photo: NASA

craters as the Moon, so asteroidal impacts have occurred numerous times since the origin of life.

The Great Jovian System: Jupiter, the giant planet of the Solar System, is made almost entirely of hydrogen, helium and a little methane. The atmospheric pressure reaches about three million times Earth's at 10,000km below the clouds where hydrogen becomes metallic, making it four times denser than water.

Earth could fit inside Jupiter over 1300 times and it is approximately 320,000 times more massive! It is probably the most interesting of all the planets to observe because it features a complex mix of yellowish, bluish and brownish gas belts that look like swirls of coloured oil paint on water in Voyager space probe pictures. The larger storm features can be seen in small telescopes. Instruments of 20cm and larger reveal exquisite detail under good seeing. Streamers can be seen connecting gas belts. Dark brownish spots of organic molecules and cocoons of white clouds form and dissipate.

An amazing Jovian feature is an enormous cyclone called the *Great Red Spot*. It is so large that Earth would fit inside it three times. In the 1960s, it

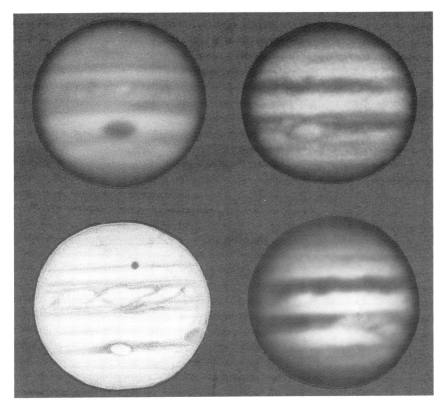

Jupiter is fascinating to observe. After only 10 minutes you can see its rapid rotation change the perspective of its features near the limb. Note the changes in shape and darkness of the gas belts and the Great Red Spot between 1971 (left) and 1984 (right). Compare the planet-wide changes between 12 June 1971 (left), 5 July 1984 (top right) and 13 September 1984 (bottom right). The drawing (bottom left) was made using a 20cm reflector at 200x on 25 May 1971. It shows the Great Red Spot disappearing around the limb and a satellite shadow transiting the disc. Photos B Adcock, Drawing: GD Thompson

was a fairly rich salmon pinkish-orange colour, but in the 1980s, high white clouds covered the pink clouds and made it the *Great White Spot*. It will no doubt become very pinkish again once the white clouds dissipate. It is interesting to make drawings of Jupiter's cloud tops to record how the different cloud bands react with the Spot and one another. Jupiter's atmosphere is extremely deep, dense and turbulent, with lightning strikes typically 2000km long. Loud, long-lasting thunder would almost certainly be heard continually over most of the planet.

Jupiter has many natural satellites but most are small captured asteroids. Its four large moons have similar sizes to Mercury and Pluto, and they can be glimpsed even in the smallest telescopes. In small apertures, they appear as stars that move around in front of, and behind, Jupiter. It is like watching a miniature Solar System in action. They frequently pass one another and cast their shadows on Jupiter (and sometimes one another), causing eclipses which appear as a jet black full stop on Jupiter. Sometimes they fade away when near Jupiter, as they disappear into its shadow. Times for such events are given in Ephemerides and astronomy magazines. A good 20cm telescope at high power under good seeing will reveal their different sizes and subtle colour differences.

The innermost moon is *Io*. Its yellowish-green surface is covered in highly active volcanoes that can spew sulphurous compounds up to hundreds of kilometres above the volcano's peak. Lakes of dark brown molasses-like sulphur lava fill the volcanoes' calderas and in some areas it floods out in rivers down to the plains. Sulphur 'icebergs' float in some lakes of molten sulphur. If you observe Io as it comes out of Jupiter's shadow, you may see that it is much brighter than usual for a minute of so before it fades back to normal brightness. In the coldness of Jupiter's shadow white sulphur snow forms and then evaporates once sunlight strikes it after coming out of the shadow.

Europa is the next moon from Jupiter. It is a pinkish-white world of ice considered to be the smoothest world in the Solar System because it is probably a frozen ocean that covers this entire world. Its impact craters are filled with water, refrozen and obliterated. Jupiter and the other moons cause tidal forces within Europa, expanding and contracting the crust and continually forming the muddy, brown cracks and ridges in the surface ice.

Travelling further from Jupiter we encounter *Ganymede,* the largest moon with a diameter of over 5000km. It takes just over seven days to orbit Jupiter; twice as long as Europa. Being covered in muddy ices it appears brownish in the eyepiece. Recent impact craters are evident in Voyager photos as white spots with bright ejecta rays. Under perfect conditions, its large dark brown markings can be glimpsed with high-powered amateur telescopes of 20cm and larger, especially when Ganymede is at its greatest western elongation from Jupiter.

Callisto is nearly as large as Ganymede and it is the furthest of the large moons from Jupiter. Callisto is yellowish white and it takes 16.7 days to orbit Jupiter. Voyager photographs show it to be peppered with small craters with clean, white ice in the interiors of the most recent impacts. The largest impact formed a huge bullseye named *Valhalla* which covers about a quarter of the surface. Callisto is mostly made of sand and ice.

The planets Jupiter, Saturn, Uranus and Neptune are giant planets of mostly gas, and are called the Gas Giant planets. They all have rings.

Majestic Saturn: Only the Moon can create the same sense of surprise that you get when you see Saturn for the first time in a telescope. Most people cannot believe it is real. Like Jupiter, Saturn has a globe that is flattened at the poles due to its rapid rotation in only ten and a half hours. It is nearly 10 times the diameter of Earth and 100 times as massive. It too is made mostly of hydrogen and helium. Like Jupiter, gas belts encircle its temperate regions but they are far less detailed, probably because of upper atmospheric hazes and Saturn's cooler interior.

In the telescope, Saturn has a yellowish-white equatorial band edged with brownish temperate gas belts and the poles appear slightly darker. Sometimes a large white storm can erupt and spread right around the belt in which it formed.

The Rings: Saturn's rings are its showpiece. The outer ring extends well over 250,000km from one side to the other. The rings vary in thickness, from 1m to 1km. They are composed of rubble in the form of ices and rocky material that range in size from powder particles to chunks as large as a bus. As the rings are tilted to the plane of the Solar System, they change their aspect to us, becoming edge-on and virtually invisible for a few months every 14 to 15 years.

Amateur telescopes show the three main rings well; however, the dark violet, inner *Crepe Ring* usually goes unnoticed by novices. It begins only several thousand kilometres above the cloud tops of Saturn. The thin, dark ring between the middle and outer rings is known as *Cassini's Division*. A good telescope and an experienced eye will show another, much thinner, and less dark ring, called *Encke's Division*, in the outer ring. It is best seen when

Saturn and its family of moons — as seen in a large amateur telescope at high power under good seeing — is the most majestic of all the planets. Note the shadow of the globe on the rings and the dark purple inner Crepe Ring.
Drawing: GD Thompson

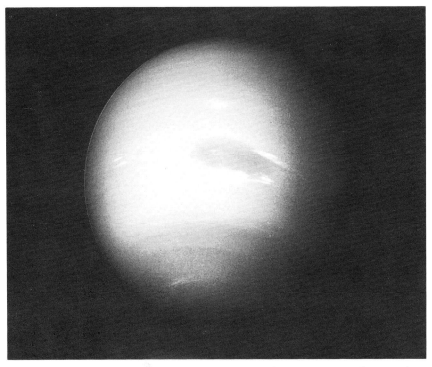

Voyager photographed Neptune's deep blue, methane gas atmosphere with its Great Dark Spot and white cirrus clouds. Photo: NASA

the rings are opened to their widest degree. Just as the globe of the planet casts a pitch-black shadow across the far side of the rings, so do the rings cast a shadow across Saturn's Equator. A 10cm telescope will show both if Saturn has a favourable aspect towards us.

Like all the Gas Giants, Saturn is surrounded by a family of moons that orbit in the same plane as the rings. A 20cm amateur telescope can usually see about seven moons and the largest moon, *Titan*, at 8th magnitude, can be seen in the smallest telescope. Like the largest moons of the other Gas Giants, Titan is actually planetary in size, being over 5000km in diameter and possessing an atmosphere one and a half times denser than Earth's. Under its orange clouds, methane rain probably falls into lakes and oceans of liquid methane. Future space probes are planned to enter the atmosphere and discover its secrets. When you see Titan beside Saturn, looking like a star, imagine that Earth would appear only about twice Titan's size.

Titan takes 16 days to move around Saturn but the five inner moons only take 1 to 4 days. Most of Saturn's other moons are icy or heavily cratered rocky worlds like our Moon. One moon, *Iapetus*, is an enigma. It is as white as snow on one side and as black as tar on the other. It can only be seen on one side of its orbit. When the dark side faces us, Iapetus becomes far too faint to see in moderate apertures.

Green Uranus: Although Uranus is fairly bright, at around magnitude 6, its disc is only about 3.5 arc seconds in diameter and it therefore requires high magnification on a telescope of 20cm or larger aperture to see it well. It displays stronger limb darkening than Jupiter, but no detail is visible. Because it has the distinction of being the only planet that rotates on its side, Uranus can show us both a face-on view of its equator and, 24 years later, a face-on view of its pole. It was probably struck by a large moon-like body early in the Solar System's formation to cause its axis to be so tilted. It is presently moving towards a polar view. When the equatorial regions were better seen, it was unmistakably yellowish green; the only object in the sky that colour. When you track down Uranus, remember that you are looking at a huge gaseous world over 50,000km in diameter and nearly 3000 million kilometres away.

Uranus has 15 known satellites of which four may be detected in large amateur telescopes with much difficulty and perseverance. One moon, *Miranda*, is most unusual. It is an icy world about 500km in diameter with sheer cliffs that are an incredible 18km straight down. It has the most tortured and diverse terrain known. It appears that a large asteroid struck Miranda and shattered it into many large fragments which over millions of years fell back together again. Parts that were originally on the inside of Miranda ended up on the outside after it reformed.

Distant Deep Blue Neptune: Neptune is 30 times as far from the Sun as Earth is: a staggering 5 billion kilometres! It is cold and dark out there. The Sun is just a bright star, yet its faint light reflects off Neptune all the way back to us, permitting us to see it as an 8th magnitude, greyish disc only 2 arc seconds in diameter. You will need at least 200x to see its disc.

Voyager photographs revealed an exquisite world with high altitude white clouds drifting over rich, ultramarine blue gases below. Like Jupiter, it displayed a *Great Dark Spot*, faint gas belts and cocoons.

Neptune has eight known moons but only its largest, *Triton*, with a diameter of 2700km, is remotely within reach of large amateur telescopes. Triton displayed an intriguing landscape to Voyager, featuring numerous, very high geysers spurting a black 'oil' that blew up to 100km downwind.

Pluto, Charon and Beyond: Revolving around the Sun at the edge of the known Solar System is the double planet, Pluto and Charon. Pluto is about 3000km in diameter and Charon is about 1000km. Pluto is so faint that a 25cm telescope is needed to see it as a very faint star. As with asteroid observations, to be sure you have seen Pluto, you will need a finder chart and once you have identified the field, plot the stars visible. Over the following nights, Pluto will become obvious by its movement.

Charon is impossibly faint and too close to Pluto to be visible in amateur scopes. Because Pluto's orbit is highly elliptical and so inclined (18°) to the plane of the other planets, Pluto and Charon may be a pair of asteroids that are the closest of a large group that form another belt beyond Neptune.

Steven Quirk tracked Comet Levy for 20 minutes in his 25cm telescope to capture the comet's blue-green coma and its blue-white gas tail (the central streaks in the tail).

Supporting this theory is the discovery in 1993 of an extremely faint and distant large asteroidal body orbiting well beyond Pluto's orbit. Many more such discoveries are expected.

Between .5 and 1 lightyear out, the *Oort Cloud* of comets is thought to exist. About 20 or so comets fall into the inner Solar System each year, where the Sun's heat can vaporise their volatile ices. As the Sun's heat shines into crevasses on the comet, it causes geyser-like eruptions of gas and dust from the comet's nucleus. Large comets, such as Halley, Bennett and West, that come close to Earth can be seen with the naked eye. Halley takes 76 years to return but most take hundreds of thousands of years, if they ever return. While the nucleus of a comet may only be kilometres in diameter, a comet's huge gaseous head (the coma) can easily measure hundreds of thousands of kilometres across and the tail frequently extends for tens of millions to hundreds of millions of kilometres across the Solar System.

When near the Sun, the coma of Comet Halley is over one million kilometres across and its tail is 200 million kilometres long, but the nucleus is a peanut-shaped asteroid-like body only 11km long by 7km wide. Its icy surface was jet black. The Giotto space probe photographed the nucleus before its camera was damaged by the impact of rubble in the inner coma.

The Nucleus of Halley's Comet
as photographed by the Giotto spacecraft

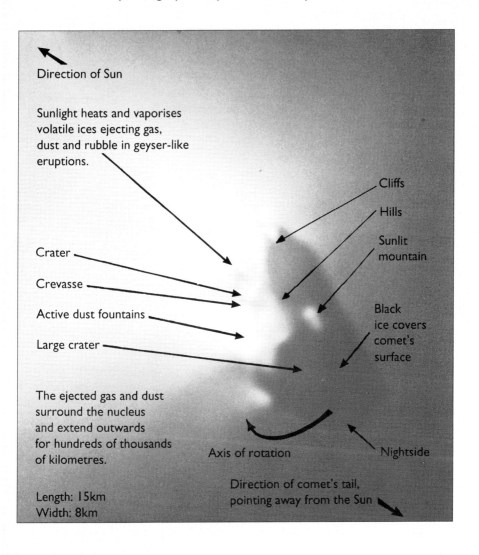

Direction of Sun

Sunlight heats and vaporises
volatile ices ejecting gas,
dust and rubble in geyser-like
eruptions.

Cliffs

Hills

Sunlit
mountain

Crater

Crevasse

Active dust fountains

Black
ice covers
comet's
surface

Large crater

The ejected gas and dust
surround the nucleus
and extend outwards
for hundreds of thousands
of kilometres.

Axis of rotation

Nightside

Length: 15km
Width: 8km

Direction of comet's tail,
pointing away from the Sun

CHAPTER SEVEN

CATCH A FALLING 'STAR'

Most people have seen 'falling' or 'shooting' stars briefly streaking across the sky. In dark country skies, meteors are seen all the time. They are micro-asteroids; tiny stones or grains of sand drifting in the Solar System that burn up as they enter the Earth's upper atmosphere some 100km above our heads. They impact with the atmosphere at around 100,000km/h or faster. The air friction makes the meteor glow white hot, and air atoms in the trail fluoresce briefly from absorbing the meteor's energy.

Most burn away within a second or two, but sometimes ones as large as a fist or a boulder are seen as extremely bright *bolides* lighting up the sky like lightning and leaving long-lasting trails. One I saw was so bright that it was as if car headlights had been turned on, making the night as bright as daylight for a few seconds. It left a bright trail that lasted for minutes. In 20 x 80 binoculars it appeared as a complicated twisted 'contrail' similar to that of a jet airliner.

Meteors the size of footballs or larger can survive their passage through the atmosphere to hit the Earth's surface, sometimes causing a sonic boom. Those that strike the surface are called *Meteorites*.

It is common to see beautiful colours such as orange, green and blue associated with meteors. The colours depend on the minerals the meteor is composed of. Flaking of the outer layers of the meteor produces small fragments that can appear to 'drip' from the head or travel beside it. Most are either carbon compounds or nearly solid iron and nickel.

If they are large enough, meteorites can cause a crater on impact. Good examples in Australia are the Henbury craters between Alice Springs and Ayres Rock, Goss' Bluff southwest of Alice and Wolf Creek Crater in northwestern Australia.

Frequently, it can be noticed over an hour or so that there are many shooting stars and they all seem to be radiating from a common point. This is called a *meteor shower*. They are caused by Earth entering a stream of debris left behind from a comet or the formation of the Solar System. Earth is thought to gain about 1000 tonnes or more of meteor dust each day and lose a similar mass of atmosphere.

This painting gives an impression of what a bright Orionids shower might look like if a few hours of meteors could be seen at once. Due to perspective, they would appear to radiate from a point, like railway lines receding into the distance. Painting by GD Thompson

CHAPTER EIGHT

WHAT STAR IS THAT?

Stars are enormous spheres of hydrogen gas that are compressed so densely in the interior that a continuous atomic reaction occurs, fusing the hydrogen into helium. The explosive force of this reaction at the centre of every sun is trying to blow the star apart but, by virtue of its huge mass, gravity is trying to crush it. A balance is achieved; at least for a few millions or billions of years. Finally, the fuel is burned and the star becomes unstable. In simple terms, if it is large enough, it can explode catastrophically as a supernova, blowing its outer gas shells away. Alternatively, if it is not so massive, it will eventually burn away to become a dull brown 'dwarf'.

Types of Stars: Some stars are as much as millions of times more voluminous than our Sun. The largest stars are called *Supergiants*, having masses in excess of 50 times the Sun and diameters 100 to 1000 times greater. Compared to the Sun, they are 10 to 20 times hotter and 10,000 to a million times brighter. The hottest supergiants, such as *Zeta Puppis*, are purplish white with surface temperatures nearing $40,000^{o}C$, while others, such as *P Cygni*, are cooler, being blue-white at around $25,000^{o}C$. *Betelgeuse* and *Antares* are much cooler, red supergiants with surface temperatures of only a few thousand degrees. They do not have distinct edges like our Sun. Supergiants' outer atmospheres are so rarefied that they fade away into space.

The next class of stars is *Giants*. They have luminosities around one hundred to several thousand times that of the Sun, with diameters of 10 to 100 times or more. One of the stars in Orion's Belt, *Delta Orionis*, is a hot, blue giant which burns its fuel so fast that it will only exist as it is for about 10 million years, whereas the Sun will burn for about 1000 times longer. *Arcturus* and *Aldebaran* are red giants about 100 times as bright as the Sun, but only half as hot.

Our Sun is a member of the most common group, the *Main Sequence* stars which have diameters between one and five times the Sun. Stars such as *Alpha Centauri* and *Procyon* are fairly similar main sequence stars to the Sun, but *Sirius*, *Regulus* and *Spica* are progressively hotter, bluer and more massive.

The next group are called *Dwarfs*. They can range from about one-tenth to as small as one-thousandth the Sun's diameter — that is much smaller than the Earth. Their masses can be one-quarter to less than one-hundredth of our Sun. White dwarf stars, such as the companions to Procyon and Sirius, are extremely dense and therefore have extremely strong gravitational fields at their surfaces. This contributes to their atmospheres being only about 30m thick as compared to the Sun's being over one million kilometres. Red dwarfs such as *Proxima Centauri* are one ten-thousandth to one-millionth as bright as the Sun and are therefore very faint indeed. Only those nearby have been discovered. All stars finally burn away to become dwarf cinders of one type or another. It is expected that dwarf stars far outnumber all other types of stars and make up much of the invisible mass in the universe. Because they are relatively cool and of low mass, they burn very slowly and are capable of lasting for over a trillion years before they become a dark star.

Also worth mentioning are two special explosive occurrences that some stars experience, known as *Novae* and *Supernovae*. Novae are thought to be associated with dwarf stars that accrete matter from a nearby companion. The dwarf heats this matter until a nuclear reaction explodes on the star's surface, thereby instantaneously increasing the dwarf's brightness many tens of thousands of times for a few days until it slowly fades back over years to its original state. Supernovae are formed by the explosion of stars 10–20 times more massive than the Sun. They occur when the inner

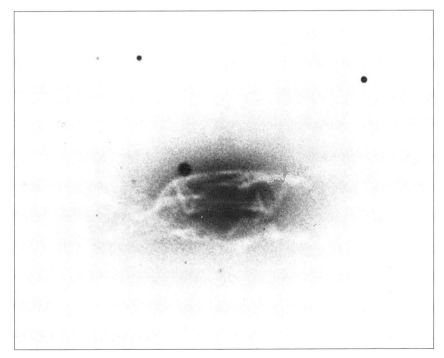

The Crossroads Galaxy, NGC 4753, displayed a supernova (top left side) in 1983 which was discovered by an Australian amateur astronomer, Rev. Robert Evans, using a 25cm homemade telescope. Photo: AAT, David Malin

core collapses after the star's fuel is burned. Gravity instantly collapses the core, which may have been millions of kilometres across, to only hundreds or tens of kilometres. Unbelievable amounts of energy are released, which explode the outer layers of the star away into the interstellar medium to possibly make new stars in the distant future. The eruption is so energetic that it alone can outshine all the other stars in the parent galaxy. While novae can rise in brightness by an average 12 magnitudes, supernovae can increase as much as 18 magnitudes.

IS IT A STAR OR A PLANET?

Venus is the brightest 'star' in the sky but it really isn't a star — it is a planet. Planets reflect the light of their sun, whereas stars radiate light by burning violently through thermonuclear reactions.

A simple way to tell a planet from a star is to note whether it twinkles. Stars twinkle: planets do not. Stars will always twinkle even a little on the steadiest nights but planets do not unless they are very low in the sky. Because planets have a disc, variations in our atmosphere's temperature, transparency and density do not cause much change in their light. Stars, however, are pinpoint sources which *are* affected by atmospheric effects. When stars are low in the sky they twinkle more than they do when they are high, simply because the air is so much thicker there and the effects are more exaggerated.

The Wanderers: The planets were called the 'wanderers' by ancient peoples because they wandered around the heavens for reasons not then understood. Today, we know that the movement of the planets is caused by their changing positions relative to one another as they orbit the Sun at different velocities.

While all the other stars in the sky appear to move across the sky from east to west during the night due to the Earth's rotation, they never move appreciably relative to one another (in our lifetimes anyway). But the planets are nearly always moving through these background stars.

The Zodiac: The planets travel across the heavens in a band of sky called the Zodiac; in the same band in which astrologer's mythological star signs are found. The Sun and the Moon also travel inside the Zodiac, which is a belt about 9° on either side of the Ecliptic — the path that the Sun traces against the background stars as viewed from Earth. The Zodiac and the Ecliptic are plotted on nearly all star atlases. The position of the midwinter and midsummer Sun marks the northern and southern limits of the Zodiac, respectively.

Where to Find the Planets: In practice, most people can recognise the planets fairly easily once they have seen them a few times. As they lie in the Zodiac, they are never very far north or south of the Celestial Equator.

We know that they move against the background stars, so if we note carefully their position we should usually see some movement from week to week and often from day to day. I say 'usually', because they can occasionally be at a stationary point for a week or so. It is interesting to plot Mars' path through the stars. Around the time Earth passes it in its orbit, Mars does a loop in the sky.

Until you are familiar with the appearance of the planets you will need to purchase a yearly *Ephemeris*. This will provide information on the positions of the planets, as well as comets, asteroids, eclipses and so on for the coming year. Most astronomical clubs have an Astronomical Yearbook. The most professional and easiest to read and use is *Astronomy Eastern Australian Edition: A Practical Guide to the Night Sky*, published by Quasar Publishing in Sydney. This publication can be obtained from most telescope shops, planetariums and various bookshops.

Colour and Brightness of the Planets: The brightness and the colour of the planets is a big help in identifying them. Venus is exceptionally bright. At magnitude -4, it is brighter than any other star or planet in the sky. It is a striking silvery white, whereas Mercury's brightness fluctuates between magnitude -1 and +1 and its colour is yellowish white.

Mars is a rust-orange colour and can look like a fire amber in the sky at its closest approach. It can be as bright as -2, but over a few months it fades to about magnitude +1.5 as it moves away from the Earth.

Jupiter is always a very bright star, surpassed only by Venus. It is usually around magnitude -2 and it has an obvious yellowish tint when compared to a white star.

Saturn is noticeably golden shining, at around magnitude 0 to +1. About every 14 years its rings are seen edge-on and unable to reflect sunlight towards us, so its brightness drops noticeably to magnitude 2. This occurs in 1995.

Uranus can just be glimpsed with the naked eye as a very faint star when it is at its closest approach to Earth. Telescopically, it has a yellowish-green tint. Neptune and Pluto are only visible in telescopes.

Coloured Stars: Many bright stars display colour differences but beginners seldom notice this. When I was a young boy, all the stars looked white. One night an amateur astronomer had me compare the colour of *Betelgeuse* with *Rigel*. By comparing them, I could immediately see that Betelgeuse was a rusty orange while Rigel was bluish white. I then compared *Sirius* and *Alpha Centaurus* and noticed that Sirius was a definite purplish white while Alpha Centaurus was yellowish.

If you want to see more really rusty orange-red stars, then look at these stars: the third and fifth brightest stars in the Southern Cross called *Gamma* and *Epsilon Crucis*, Betelgeuse in Orion, *Antares* in Scorpius, *Arcturus* in Bootes and *Aldeberan* in Taurus.

In the northern winter sky, you will find a 3rd magnitude star marked on maps as *Albireo (Beta Cygnus)*, near the southern tip of Cygnus. In a moderate aperture telescope at low power, it is one of the sky's most beautiful double stars. Sitting together is a bright steel-blue star beside a strong golden yellow one.

This double is typical of numerous other doubles with coloured components all over the sky. When a cloud of interstellar gas condenses, it clumps into many swirling condensations with the most massive at the centre which becomes the central sun. If some of the other clumps orbiting the central star are massive enough, they too will become suns. Less massive condensations become planets, asteroids and interplanetary dust. The gravity of planets tend to attract smaller objects, thereby sweeping up much of the debris in the system.

The reddest star I have ever seen is around magnitude 10, so it needs a telescope to see it. It is easy to find because it lies right beside the second brightest star in the Southern Cross, *Beta Crucis*. Beta, too, is a double consisting of two brilliant, hot, purplish-white stars. In the same field of view can be seen this much cooler, ruby red, carbon star.

The colour of a star tells us how hot it is. An analogy is when we heat iron. It first starts to glow dull red, then it glows orange. As we heat it further, it becomes bright yellow and then dazzling white. Stars are similar. Red stars are relatively cool at about 3000K, yellow stars such as the Sun are warmer at around 6000K, white stars are around 10,000K, blue stars are a hot 20,000K and violet stars can be an extremely torrid 30,000K. (The temperature measurement 'K' is for Kelvin. Zero degrees K is when there's no energy whatsoever. It is so cold that theoretically, electrons would stop orbiting their atomic nucleus.)

The Brightest Stars: The sky is divided unequally into 88 regions which are called constellations. The brighter stars in some constellations vaguely represent forms derived from ancient folklore. Once you know the brightest stars in the sky, you will find that recognition of the constellations comes as a natural second step. Learning which stars are which can only be done using a star map under the stars or having a personal instructor.

There are almost 100 stars brighter than magnitude 2 and the bulk of these lie in the southern sky. The brightest star in a constellation takes the designation Alpha represented by this symbol 'α', which is the first letter in the Greek alphabet. The second brightest is represented by 'β' Beta, the second letter, and the third by 'γ' Gamma, the third letter and so on. So, it is no surprise that the 21 brightest stars in the Table of Brightest Stars on page 61 are all represented by either an Alpha or Beta designation.

GREEK ALPHABET

Alpha	α	Epsilon	ε	Iota	ι	Nu	ν	Rho	ρ	Phi	φ
Beta	β	Zeta	ζ	Kappa	κ	Xi	ξ	Sigma	σ	Chi	χ
Gamma	γ	Eta	η	Lambda	λ	Omicron	o	Tau	τ	Psi	ψ
Delta	δ	Theta	θ	Mu	μ	Pi	π	Upsilon	υ	Omega	ω

Stars with Variable Brightness: There are numerous stars that have been found to vary in brightness — some vary wildly while others have subtle changes. Some are as regular as clockwork and other types are completely unpredictable.

Astrophysicists have deduced many reasons for this. When a bright star orbits a duller, often larger star, the bright star can be eclipsed as it travels behind its companion, thereby causing the light of the two stars to drop in brightness. *Eclipsing Binaries,* as they are called, have very regular changes. Other stars are thought to have brightness variations on their surfaces that change irregularly, probably from huge sunspot storms or flares.

Some stars have close companions. Matter can stream from one star to the other. This ultimately builds up to an extremely brilliant outburst of energy over a few hours then a slow fading until the next outburst months or decades later. This class is referred to as *Cataclysmic Variables.* Novae, which can have outbursts that increase 7 to 16 magnitudes, are the extreme of this type. Very large stars tend to pulsate slightly in brightness with periods from one month to one and a half years. A classic example is *Mira,* in the constellation Cetus. Every 11 months Mira rises in brightness from magnitude 10 to 2.5, and once it reached 1.2. This is an excellent naked-eye and binocular variable to photograph its brightness changes or simply watch it disappear and reappear. Keep a note of how bright it is every week in a notebook by comparing it to other nearby stars.

TABLE OF BRIGHTEST STARS

	Name	Bayer Designation	Visual Magnitude	Distance in Light Years
1	Sirius	α Canis Majoris	-1.46	8.6
2	Canopus	α Carinae	-0.72	100
3	Rigil Kentaurus	α Centauri	-0.27	4.5
4	Acturus	α Bootis	-0.04	36
5	Vega	α Lyrae	+.03	26
6	Capella	α Aurigae	+0.08	45
7	Rigel	β Orionis	+0.12	900
8	Procyon	α Canis Minoris	+0.38	11.4
9	Archernar	α Eridani	+0.46	90
10	Betelgeuse	α Orionis	+0.50 (var)	300
11	Hadar	β Centauri	+0.61	520
12	Altair	α Aquilae	+0.77	17
13	Aldebaran	α Tauri	+0.85 (var)	68
14	Acrux	α Crucis	+0.87	370
15	Antares	α Scorpii	+0.96 (var)	500
16	Spica	α Virginis	+0.98	220
17	Pollux	β Geminorum	+1.14	35
18	Fomalhaut	α Piscis Austrini	+1.16	83
19	Deneb	α Cygni	+1.25	1600
20	Mimosa	β Crucis	+1.25	470
21	Regulus	α Leonis	+1.35	85
22	Ahara	ε Canis Major	+1.42	650
23	Bellitrix	γ Orionis	+1.61	450

CHAPTER NINE

IDENTIFYING MAJOR CONSTELLATIONS AND BRIGHT STARS

There are really only two constellations that look vaguely like their mythological names would suggest. The most obvious are *Scorpius* 'the Scorpion' and *Orion* 'the Hunter'. For the others you need to stretch your imagination. Nevertheless, they can be easily recognised as geometric shapes. If you know some of the bright and easy ones, then you can soon find the fainter ones using a star atlas. A basic star atlas or a planisphere will enable you to find those of the 88 constellations visible from your latitude.

Around 9pm in mid-January we can find some easy-to-identify summer constellations. They are particularly beautiful in a clear dark moonless sky away from stray lights.

Begin by looking just north of overhead at the *Saucepan*. This seems to be a star group that most people know. It is actually the central part of *Orion*. The three bright stars along the saucepan's base are 'Orion's Belt', while the three faint stars forming the handle of the saucepan are 'Orion's Sword'. The orange-red supergiant Betelgeuse, 8° to the north, forms Orion's head while Rigel, a little below the sword, marks his foot.

If Betelgeuse were at the centre of our Solar System, it would fill it to halfway between Jupiter and Saturn. It lies about 300 lightyears away. Betelgeuse varies slightly in brightness, which is thought to be caused by huge dark sunspots forming in its photosphere deep inside its extremely tenuous outer atmosphere.

About a hand span southeast of Orion's Belt is the lord of all stars, *Sirius*. Sirius is the brightest star *in the night sky*. It shines brilliantly at magnitude -1.46. Over the summer evenings, it stands proud, high in the sky, 16° south of the Celestial Equator culminating at midnight on 1 January.

Sirius, 'The Sparkling One', belongs to the constellation *Canis Major*, meaning 'The Big Dog'. It is often called the 'Dog Star'. It is more than

The Summer Sky:

The most obvious stars and constellations

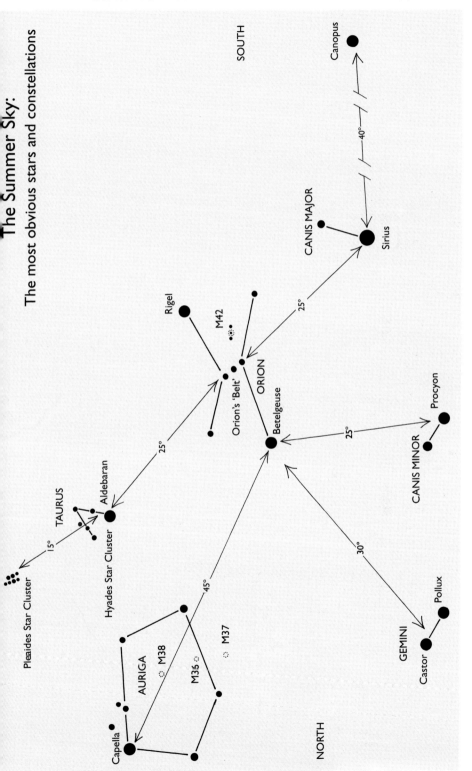

The constellations of Canis Major and Canis Minor lie across the centre.
Sirius, the brightest star in the sky, is below centre and Procyon is above
centre. The summer Milky Way passes diagonally between them. Orion is at
right with the three 'Belt' stars close together with Orion's Sword immediately
below. The supergiant Betelgeuse is the bright star at the far right of Orion
and Rigel is at its top. Photo: A Fujii

20 times as luminous as our Sun and nearly twice its diameter. It lies rather close to us at only 9 lightyears, being the 9th nearest star known. Sirius has a companion star orbiting it once every 50 years. It is a white dwarf star estimated to be only ⅟₅₀th the diameter of our Sun or about 2.5 times larger than our Earth yet its mass approximately equals our Sun's! A matchbox full of it would weigh thousands of tonnes.

A hand span northeast of Betelgeuse you will see the bright red star *Aldebaran*, the brightest star in *Taurus*. It forms the 'Eye of the Bull', and around it you will see a V-shape of stars pointing westwards. This is the *Hyades* cluster. A little further northwest are the *Seven Sisters* or the *Pleiades* cluster, which also looks like a small saucepan with a large and small handle on each side.

Low on the northern horizon is *Capella*, the 6th brightest star in the sky. Together with six other bright stars that form a distorted pentagon-like shape, they form the constellation *Auriga*. If your sky is dark, you will see the summer Milky Way as a faint irregular haze to the east of Orion and Taurus and running through Auriga.

Eta Carinae Nebula as it is seen in large binoculars. Note the relatively small, [elon]gated and very dark nebula on its southern (bottom) edge. The star cluster NGC [?] in the top left corner is probably the richest telescopic cluster in the sky for small [teles]copes. The bright spot to the top right of the nebula is the bright compact cluster [NG]C 3293. Photo D Gooden

[c]entral portion of the Eta Carinae Nebula. This illustrates the type of view visible [in m]oderate sized amateur telescopes. The Keyhole Nebula is the dark, curly intrusion [in th]e bright section at the top. South is at the bottom in these views. Photo S Quirk

The Great Orion Nebula (M42) blazes in the reddish light of ionised hydrogen while its companion nebula NGC 1977 is a beautiful blue dust nebula, reflecting the light from the nearby stars. Photo S Quirk

This photograph was taken using a 25cm reflector and hypersensitised film. The Trifid Nebula displays pinkish hydrogen emission nebulosity, blue reflection nebulosity as well as three dark nebulous veins that give rise to its name. Photo S Quirk

The northern summer sky rewards us with two superb naked-eye star clusters, both in the constellation of Taurus. The larger is the Hyades, surrounding the giant red star Aldaberan, and the smaller is the Pleiades, commonly known as the Seven Sisters. Photo: A Fujii

Due east of Betelgeuse and on the other side of the Milky Way is *Canis Minor* 'the Small Dog'. This constellation's brightest star, *Procyon*, is the 8th brightest star in the sky. A hand span due north of Procyon is the constellation *Gemini* with its 'twins', the bright stars *Castor* and *Pollux*, which are only 4° apart. Castor is a double, double, double star. In a small telescope at high power, it resolves into two close stars of nearly equal brightness. By analysing the light from both these stars, the world's largest telescopes have shown that both these stars are double as well. If that's not enough, one of those stars has been found to be double also. To top it all off, a more distant companion orbits the lot!

Two hand spans south of Sirius we see the second brightest star in the sky, *Canopus*, in the constellation *Carina*. Sirius and Canopus are often used by spacecraft for navigation. Canopus is extraordinarily bright, estimated to be 7000 times as bright as the Sun. Its light shines across 200 lightyears to reach us. With a diameter at least 30 times that of the Sun — about as large as Mercury's orbit — it is one of the most luminous supergiants known.

South of Sirius, along the Milky Way, we pass through the constellations of *Puppis, Vela* and *Carina*. This region has the highest concentration of bright stars in the sky. Here we find the *False Cross*, which consists of four,

2nd magnitude stars on the border of Vela and Carina. The False Cross is about half as large again as the *Southern Cross*. The Southern Cross, known as the constellation *Crux*, is 35° southeast of the False Cross. Note that, going clockwise, each of the five stars of the Southern Cross is fainter than the preceding one.

The constellation *Centaurus* surrounds Crux. *Alpha Centauri* is the 3rd brightest star in the sky and it is the brightest of *The Pointers* — the two stars that point to the Southern Cross. Alpha Centauri is a striking, double star that is easy to resolve (separate into two) in a small telescope. It lies in a Milky Way field strewn with numerous fainter stars. Its two suns are very similar in size, temperature and colour to our Sun. These two stars are connected gravitationally. They are, on average, about the same distance apart as Uranus is from the Sun. A faint (14.5) red dwarf star called *Proxima Centauri* appears to be in a huge orbit around both stars.

Around 9pm in mid-November the Milky Way lies all the way around the horizon in Australia. The Southern Cross is touching the southern horizon and the *Large Magellanic Cloud* (see Chapter 16) is culminating 20° above the SCP. *Achernar* lies 15° above the Large Cloud. A little over one and a half hand spans to the northwest is the bright star *Fomalhaut*, high in the sky. There are not many bright stars in this region because we are looking out below the thin arms of our galaxy and not through them as we do when we look along the Milky Way. The constellation *Grus* is about a hand span south of Fomalhaut. It is easy to recognise as its most prominent section looks like a 'Y' upside down, with a couple of doubles along its 'tail' visible to the naked eye.

Around 9pm in late April *Arcturus* blazes in the northeastern sky. It is the dominating, reddish star in the constellation *Bootes*, being the brightest star in the northern sky. At 35 lightyears, it is the nearest giant to us. Arcturus is rather large, being more than 20 times the diameter of the Sun, but it is only four times as massive because its large outer layers are extremely rarefied.

Regulus, the brightest star of the constellation *Leo*, shines in the northwest. Leo looks more like a sickle in the sky than a lion. Regulus forms the top of the sickle handle with the blade hanging below to the north. The brightest star in the constellation *Virgo* is called *Spica*. It is virtually overhead and noticeably bluish. A distorted 'square' of 3rd magnitude stars, one and a half fists from Spica, is the obvious constellation *Corvus*. The well-known northern constellation, the *Big Dipper*, straddles the northern horizon. It is only really visible from the northern half of the continent.

In April, we see the sky that lies *above* the plane of the Milky Way. As there are no spiral arms in the way when we look above and below the arms of our galaxy, we can see far out into the universe, enabling us to view hundreds of other galaxies in moderate apertures.

The Scorpion and the Teapot

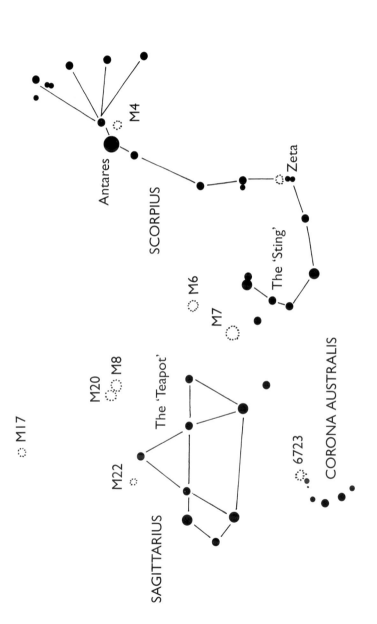

Around 9pm in early August is a nice time to see the rich winter constellations along the brightest parts of the Milky Way. *Sagittarius* is directly overhead. Once they are pointed out, the brightest stars resemble a geometric 'teapot'. The bright centre of the Milky Way is situated here. *Scorpius* lies immediately to the west, with its 'Sting' hooked in the Milky Way.

The bright red star *Antares* is at the centre of the Scorpion's body. Antares is so large it would reach all the way to the Asteroid Belt between Mars and Jupiter if it replaced the Sun. It is a remarkable double star. A good, high-powered telescope on a steady night will show its intensely blue, 6.5 magnitude companion Antares B, almost lost in its glare. An occulting bar placed over the field stop of a high magnification eyepiece can be used to hide Antares to make the companion easier to see. Even though the two stars seem so close, Antares B orbits Antares A at a distance equal to about six times the radius of Pluto's orbit. The region of dust that envelopes this star system appears reddish due to the light reflected from the supergiant Antares A.

A hand span north of the Celestial Equator in the Milky Way lies the bright star *Altair*, guarded by a star on either side. It is the principal star of the constellation *Aquila*. In the far northern sky is the magnificent constellation *Cygnus* — 'the Swan'. It looks like an ibis in flight or a sword. The brightest star, *Deneb*, lies at the base of the handle of the sword or the ibis's feet, while the bright stars above Deneb, running at right angles to it, are the hand guard of the sword or the wings of the bird. The two fainter stars that reach high into the sky are the blade of the sword or the bird's neck and head. The colourful double *Albireo* is the tip of the sword or the bird's head.

Deneb is special because it is the most luminous star visible from our sector of the galaxy. It is calculated to be an astonishing 60,000 times brighter than our Sun. If it were as near as Sirius it would be blindingly bright. It has a mass equal to 30 Suns and a diameter about the size of the Earth's orbit.

About 25° to the west is the magnificent star *Vega*, the 5th brightest in the sky and the brightest star of the constellation *Lyra*. Above Vega is a parallelogram of four 3rd and 4th magnitude stars. The *Ring Nebula* lies between the top two stars.

If you can identify no more than the bright stars and constellations mentioned in this chapter, then you will find it easy to star-hop, with the aid of a star atlas, to anywhere in the sky.

CHAPTER TEN

DISCOVERING THE GLORIOUS MILKY WAY

To me, the most impressive view of anything astronomical is the winter Milky Way as seen with the naked eye. No telescopic object or even a Total Solar Eclipse can deliver so much detail across the entire sky.

What Is the River of Light? The Egyptians called the Milky Way a *River of Light*. It can look like thin cloud to the uneducated eye. When a pair of binoculars or a telescope is trained on this 'haze', it becomes apparent what it really is — billions of stars. They are so far away that they appear to be almost on top of one another. They are too faint to be seen individually with the naked eye, but their combined light becomes the Milky Way: the galaxy in which we live.

How to View Our Galaxy: Nowadays, to see this awe-inspiring sight at its best, we must unfortunately travel to the country to escape urban sky glow. If you are camping in a national park, perhaps visiting a friend's farm or have simply stopped along an outback highway, get right away from stray lights or fires so that you can achieve maximum dark adaption (see Chapter 4) to fully appreciate this wonderful spectacle.

A great time to see our galaxy at its best is around midnight in May or 9pm in July. At this time, it stretches from Vela on the southwestern horizon up through rich Carina, past the Southern Cross and the Pointers in Centaurus, high into the southern sky through Scorpius and Sagittarius at the galaxy's centre and then down through the Scutum Star Cloud and finally into Cygnus over the northeastern horizon.

Our galaxy looks very similar to the *Great Andromeda Galaxy*. It measures about 100,000 lightyears across. To make this immense distance comprehensible, imagine our galaxy is the size of Australia. Even at this scale, its thousand billion stars would be almost invisible specks about

The Great Andromeda Galaxy, M31, is a superb example of a spiral galaxy similar to our own. Like the Milky Way, it too has small satellite galaxies such as the hazy sphere M32 (below centre right). Photo: M Germano

200m apart. Our entire Solar System would only measure 20mm across and we would need a super, high-powered tunnelling microscope to find Earth. Don't even try to think about how small we are. And to think our galaxy is but a minuscule speck itself in a never-ending universe filled with galaxies!

Getting it in Perspective: To truly appreciate our view of the galaxy, lie down under a dark, cloud-free sky, turn on some relaxing, meditative music, remember to use averted vision and take a little mind journey first. Close your eyes for a moment and try to visualise being out in intergalactic space well below our spiral galaxy looking up at its central hub and its winding arms filled with billions of stars and clouds of bright gas and dark dust. There are no stars visible anywhere in your imaginary sky from this intergalactic location. From here, the galaxy is a soft misty glow brightening towards the centre.

Now imagine you are zooming up into the spiral arms two-thirds of the way from the centre. Your imagination will permit you to travel at millions of times the speed of light. Slow to a halt and open your eyes and take in this awe-inspiring sight. You have stopped exactly where the Sun resides in the Orion Arm of the Milky Way, just below it is the centre. You are now surrounded by stars in every direction but naturally there is a

This amazing view of a part of the Cigar Galaxy, NGC 55, taken by David Malin with the Anglo-Australian Telescope, is probably very similar to how our galaxy appears edge-on. Astronomers studying NGC 55 with the AAT can use such high magnifications that individual clusters can fill the telescope's TV monitor, enlarging the galaxy's image to 3.5m long. Photo: AAT

concentration towards the disc of the galaxy where they all reside. Only stars relatively close to you appear above and below the plane of the Milky Way.

In winter, you peer through the clouds of stars and dust lanes to see some of the Sagittarius Arm, the arm inside ours. Much more difficult to see at all is the Centaurus arm which lies still closer to the centre. In summer, when we look outwards, away from the centre, we see a fainter band of Milky Way stretching across the sky. This is the *Perseus Arm*.

Our winter view looks in towards the galactic hub at the centre 30,000 lightyears away, but we cannot see it because it is hidden behind spiral arms of dark interstellar dust clouds.

Dust Lanes — Incubators of Life?: Look along the Milky Way and you will notice dark winding streaks that appear like 'holes' in this heavenly spectacle. These are the galaxy's dust lanes; enormous clouds of dark dust and gas floating in the arms of the galaxy. Stars, planets, asteroids, comets and so on are believed to condense out of this matter.

Astronomers using Australia's Parkes Radio Telescope discovered that organic molecules — the building blocks of life — exist in these clouds. There is mounting evidence that life may be a natural consequence of the evolution of the universe. It is likely that it teems with great diversity throughout the universe as it does on Earth. It does not follow, however, that advanced lifeforms could visit us. The problems associated with overcoming the huge distances involved together with physical impossibility of not being able to travel faster than light, are insurmountable, even for the most advanced, long-living civilisations.

The obvious dark nebula on the eastern side of the Southern Cross is called the *Coal Sack*. It is dense enough to blot out almost all the background stars. If you look at the centre of the galaxy in Sagittarius from a dark site, you will notice other complex areas of intertwining dust clouds crisscrossing the background Milky Way. Binoculars show this very well and photographs reveal their nature even more so.

Notice how the dust lanes gravitate more towards the western side of the Milky Way. This is because our Sun is situated on the eastern side, a little below the centre of the spiral arm. (That is, we are just south of the plane of the galaxy.) The distant Milky Way star clouds can be seen 'under' the dust clouds, which are projecting towards us and hiding much of the Milky Way above the galaxy's arms.

The Milky Way's Hot Spots: All along the Milky Way are what look like hazy concentrations. These are mostly large, bright clusters of stars too faint to be seen individually, or bright gaseous nebulae. A most obvious 'hot spot' is in the centre of Carina. It is the huge *Eta Carinae Nebula*. In the photograph of Eta Carinae it shows as a red object to the right-hand edge surrounded by some blue and white star clusters. (See Chapter 12.)

This wide-angle photograph illustrates beautifully a typical naked-eye view of the winter Milky Way from Vela to Sagittarius. Note how obvious the dust lanes are silhouetted against the misty light of the millions of stars that form the spiral arms. The sky is so transparent in this wide-angle photo, taken at Mt Magnet in Western Australia, that stars can be seen right to the horizon. The two detached clouds above the horizon are the Magellanic Clouds, galaxies that orbit the Milky Way. The stars that form the Scorpion's claws as well as Antares are at centre top, while the Pointers are right of centre and the Southern Cross and the Eta Carinae Nebula are to the right. The picture shows the Australian Aborigines' Great Emu in the sky, formed by the dust lanes. The head is formed by the Coal Sack, with the beak being the pointed portion. The emu's eye is the 6th magnitude star embedded in it. The emu's neck is formed by the rift running from Alpha Centauri through the constellation Norma. The body and wings are formed from the broad, complex dust lanes drifting across Scorpius and Sagittarius. The legs and feet run to the border of Scutum and Aquila. The bird is standing upright. The bright star below the galaxy's centre is not on any star atlas — it is Jupiter. Photo: A Fujii

Unfortunately, the brightness of the Milky Way is too low for the eye to detect colour, but fast colour film can. Note that in colour photographs the semitranslucent dust is a brownish colour. Interstellar dust absorbs all but red light.

Viewing the Outer Edge: The summer Milky Way is not as bright or as complex but it, too, is truly magnificent, albeit more serene.

Midnight in December or early evening in late January are good times to see the summer Milky Way. At this time, the Southern Cross and the Pointers are rising in the southeast, Sirius is overhead, Orion is a little north of the zenith and Capella is low in the north.

Our summer view looks in the opposite direction to our winter view: we look towards the outer edge of our galaxy's spiral arms, about 20,000 lightyears away. As there are far fewer stars towards the outer edge of the Milky Way, it is not as bright as looking towards the centre in winter.

Along the Milky Way from the Southern Cross, through Vela, and on to Puppis, are many unresolved, naked-eye star clusters. Binoculars show them like tailless comets. *M41* is easy, being only 5° south of Sirius. Close to the northern horizon, Auriga sports three star clusters of which some are faintly visible to the naked eye and well seen in binoculars. From Brisbane northwards, the 'Big W' of *Cassiopeia* in the far northern Milky Way can be seen just clearing a low northern horizon and a clear sky will show the famous *Perseus Double Cluster* close by.

CHAPTER ELEVEN

FLUORESCENT GAS, REFLECTIVE STARDUST AND DARK NEBULAE

Floating in the spiral arms of the galaxy are hundreds of major clouds of diffuse gas and dust called *nebulae*, that range up to hundreds of lightyears in size. From our location in the galaxy, we can only see the relatively nearby ones, because those far away are obscured by star clouds and dust.

These nebulae are the birthplaces of the stars. Portions of these clouds condense over millions of years to form new stars and, presumably, planets. There are three main types of nebulae: Ionised Gaseous Emission Nebulae, Dust Reflection Nebulae and Dark Nebulae.

Ionised Gaseous Emission Nebulae glow or fluoresce just as neon tubes do. Ionised hydrogen, often referred to as HII, glows reddish orange, while ionised oxygen glows in a yellowish-green light. Very hot ultraviolet stars heat the gas to around 10,000K, exciting the gas atoms to emit light. Old astronomical films were more sensitive to red and blue light than green. This is the reason why green nebulae are rarely ever seen in astronomy book photographs. Modern films are more balanced, capturing more of oxygen's green hues.

Dust Reflection Nebulae are formed from nearby starlight reflecting off dust particles, similar to cigarette smoke. Cigarette smoke looks bluish when light reflects off it, especially when it is seen against a dark background, yet it looks reddish brown when viewed against a light background. Similarly, interstellar dust particles reflect blue light, in addition to reddening and attenuating starlight passing through them.

Dark Nebulae are clouds of gas and dust that are *not* illuminated due to a lack of nearby stars. They are usually only seen when projected against a bright background (for example, a bright nebula) or detected by their effect of reddening starlight.

(Another special type of gaseous emission nebulae, called *Planetary Nebulae*, is discussed separately in Chapter 13.)

Often two types of diffuse nebulae can be seen in the one object, and occasionally all three. Some of the best examples of all types are high in the southern sky.

The *Eta Carinae Nebula* is the most impressive. It is so bright that it can be seen with the naked eye as a smudge of light in the Milky Way in Carina.

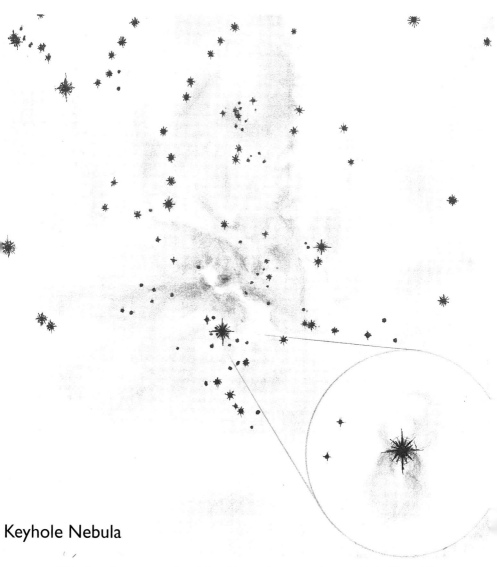

Keyhole Nebula

This drawing was made with a 32cm telescope using an OIII filter. The Homunculus Nebula (inset) is drawn at 660x to reveal its looped structure around the star Eta Carinae. Drawing: GD Thompson

Surrounded by several spectacular, naked-eye star clusters, lying within only 10°, the outer regions of Eta Carinae spread to four times the diameter of the Moon. Because it is so huge, many small clusters of stars have been born within its gas clouds.

Its declination is almost the same as the Pointers, and it lies about the same distance west of the Southern Cross as the Pointers are east. In star atlases, the nebula is often marked as the Greek symbol for Eta.

Binoculars show its hazy appearance well. Telescopically, it is simply stunning. Filling the field, even at low power, it is divided into two main sections by the *Great Rift* — a dark L shaped nebula that is silhouetted across the bright central regions. Close inspection of the central regions with a telescope of 20cm aperture and larger, using medium to high power, is breathtaking, particularly when a UHC or OIII filter is used.

The edge of the Great Rift is serrated by dark notches and small bays. Near the elbow of the rift lies the famous *Keyhole Nebula*, which is actually a dark dust nebula, superimposed onto the bright centre of the nebula. In the same field of view is the bright, enigmatic star *Eta*, after which the nebula was named. It is thought to be a recurring nova. Some centuries ago, it was a naked-eye star that fluctuated in brightness between magnitudes 4 and 1, but, in 1843, Eta Carinae reached -1, being outshone only by Sirius. While presently a telescopic variable star, it could rise to great brilliance again at any time. Eta is very orange. Look at it with very high power and you will not be able to bring it to a pinpoint focus like the other stars around it. This is because it is enveloped in an intense nebulosity called the *Homunculus Nebula* or *Loop Nebula* (inset in the drawing), which is half a lightyear across and rapidly expanding.

The *Great Orion Nebula*, also known as M42, is a spectacular nebulosity. Together with some telescopic stars surrounding it, M42 appears so bright that it can be seen with the naked eye as the middle, fuzzy 'star' in the Sword of Orion. In the telescope, it displays an intense white core into which a complex, dark, squarish nebula intrudes. At the very core are exceptionally fine examples of very hot O-type stars that emit energetic, ultraviolet light that excites the surrounding gas, making it fluoresce. These four stars are close together and are known as the *Trapezium*. The 3rd brightest is calculated to be as brilliant as 400,000 suns. If you look carefully with high power, you will see that two of the Trapezium stars are double. In 40cm reflectors, the nebula is bright enough to begin to show colour visually. The inner sections take on a bluish-green tint and the outstretched 'wings' become a rusty orange colour. M42 is estimated to be about 1600 lightyears away. Directly north in the same low-powered field is *M43*, a bluish reflection nebula.

The *Omega Nebula* or *Swan Nebula*, also known as M17, looks distinctly like a swan. It glows rich red when photographed. M17 displays the most contrast of all nebulae and is superb when viewed through an OIII filter, testifying to it possessing an abundance of oxygen.

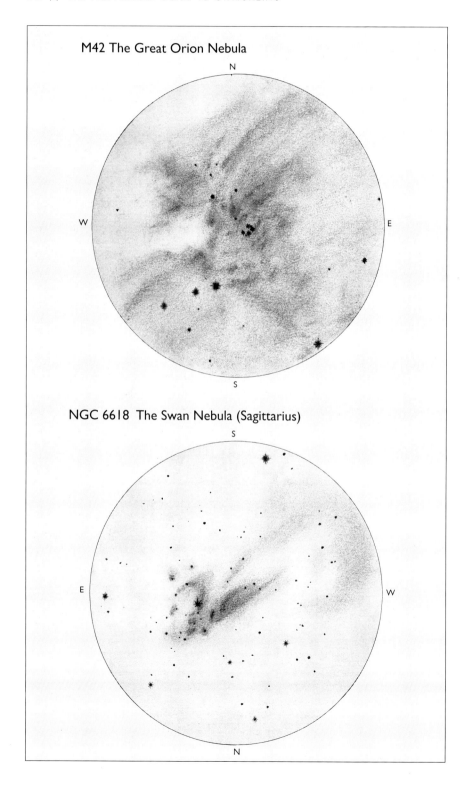

The Lagoon Nebula is visible to the naked eye as a hazy spot, but telescopically it displays dark rifts, a superimposed star cluster and Bok Globules of dark matter presumably condensing into other solar systems. Photo: S Quirk

Above: The Hourglass Nebula lies at the centre of the brightest portion of the Lagoon Nebula. Due to its small dimensions, it needs high magnification to see it at its best. Photo: J Marling, using the 64cm reflector at Mauna Kea Observatory

Opposite: The extremely hot ultraviolet stars of the 'Trapezium' star group show well at the centre of M42 in this drawing made at 330x. Bottom: The 'Swan' Nebula is a high contrast nebula rich in ionised oxygen. The shape that gives it its name shows well in this drawing at 187x. Both sketches are by the author using a 32cm reflector.

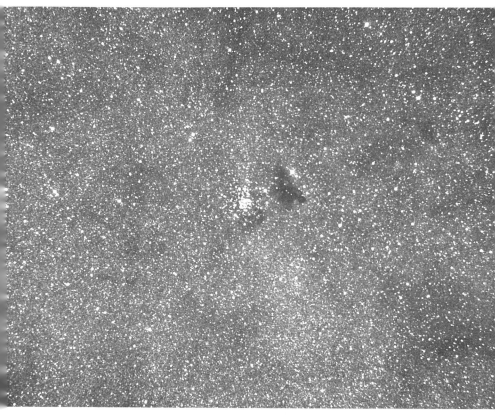

This is the 86th entry in Barnard's list of dark nebulae. The background stars are packed so tightly in the direction of the Milky Way's centre that they seem to overlap one another, making B86 very obvious. Photo: S Quirk

The *Lagoon Nebula*, M8, needs a low-powered eyepiece so that its large ½° form can contrast against the dark surrounding sky. This wonderful object is situated in a very rich Milky Way field. It has many features, such as the star cluster *NGC 6530*, near its centre. An interesting dark nebula winds gracefully right across its brighter regions. High magnification reveals a bright core that is aptly called the *Hourglass Nebula*. Large apertures detect a number of very small dark 'globules', particularly towards the edges. Its distance is computed to be a little less than 5000 lightyears.

The *Trifid Nebula*, M20, is not as bright or large as M8. It lies only a couple of degrees north of M8. The dark lanes are not easy to see unless a telescope of at least 20cm is used. M20 magnificently displays a blue reflection nebula directly behind the pinkish HII region. The Trifid lies at the same distance as M8.

Barnard 86 is probably the densest and most well-defined dark nebula to observe in a telescope. A delicate star cluster, *NGC 6520* lies on one side and a red star to its other.

bright star is Zeta Orionis, the eastern-most star in Orion's Belt and below it is the
nge Christmas Tree Nebula, NGC 2024, strongly resembling a fur tree. To the right
e small blue reflection nebula whose faint light is often mistaken for glare from the
edded star. Above is the Horsehead Nebula silhouetted against a veil of red
ground nebulosity. It appears bright in photographs, but is actually small and faint,
iring a large aperture telescope and a Hydrogen Beta filter to see it well. Photo S Quirk

y a degree northwest of Eta Carina is the exquisite Diamonds and Rubies Cluster,
C 3293. It takes one by surprise when its brilliant compact sphere of red and blue
 enters the field of view. Around the cluster can be seen the remains of the blue dust
 which it formed. NGC3324 is the pink arcing nebulosity to the north (right).
S Quirk

The central star of the Helix Nebula, NGC 7293 expanded and shed its outer layers t *form this enormous gas ring more than a lightyear in diameter.* Photo S Quirk

The Dumbbell Nebula is a spectacular, bright planetary nebula which is easy to dete *in small telescopes as a hazy orb in the constellation of Vulpecula.* Photo J Marling

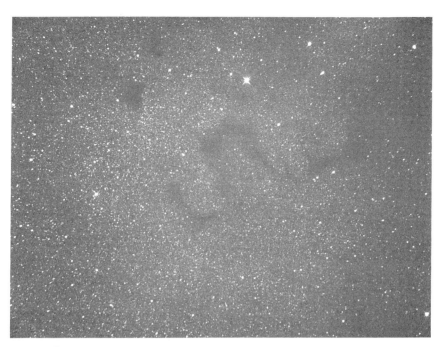

Barnard 72 is an S-shaped dark nebula in Ophiuchus.

The 'Southern Crown', Corona Australis features this extraordinary region displaying dark nebulosity, variable stars, variable bright nebulae and a fine globular cluster. Photos: S Quirk

A binocular view of the Seven Sisters shows many more stars than the seven or so that can be seen with the naked eye. Photo: T Hunter

A small telescope shows a profusion of hundreds of fainter stars surrounding the bright naked-eye members. Note the very faint reflection nebula around the brightest stars. Photo: S Quirk

Barnard 72 and *68* are harder to detect than B86, but are interesting because of the distinctive S-shape, which is followed by the dark 'full stop' appearance of B68. You will need large binoculars or a 20cm aperture at very low power in a dark sky to see these dark nebulae well.

An area of sky that is fascinating because of its complexity and diversity of objects, lies in the constellation *Corona Australis*, the Southern Crown. This small constellation is a half circle of about a dozen stars of 4th and 5th magnitude immediately south of Sagittarius. Along the northern edge of Corona Australis lies a large area of dark nebulosity that completely blacks out all the rich Milky Way field stars. At the western edge is a remarkable pair of bright nebulae that vary in brightness, NGC 6726/27/29. NGC 6726 and 6727 form a bright figure 8-shaped nebula that surrounds a double star. One component star of this double is magnitude 7.2, while the other is an erratic variable fluctuating between 8.8 and 12.5. Only 5 arc minutes southeast is a fainter, comet-shaped nebula NGC 6729, the 'head' of which also has an erratic variable star changing by up to 3 magnitudes. These light changes effect not only the brightness of the nebula's 'tail' but its shape as well. Fast-moving dust clouds are perhaps drifting in front of the star, casting shadows across the tail. To top off the whole region, a beautiful, rich globular cluster, *NGC 6723*, lies in the same low-powered field.

CHAPTER TWELVE

OUR GALAXY'S STELLAR JEWEL BOXES

*G*alactic Star Clusters, also called *Open Star Clusters*, are groups of stars that typically contain as little as 20 stars or as many as a few hundred. (For reasons unknown, some other galaxies, such as the Large Magellanic Cloud, have open clusters that are several times as populous.) Stars frequently form in clusters within the spiral arms where they are born from the same cloud of gas. Once born, their radiation pressure blows away most of the remaining gas. The *Rosette Nebula* is an excellent example of this. They tend to stay together for a long time after they have formed but seldom more than two rotations around the galaxy's centre. The following are a small selection of clusters that comprise some of the most beautiful in the sky.

The largest of all open clusters is fairly easily visible to the naked eye. Its brightest members form the constellation *Coma Berenices*. The next largest is the *Hyades*. About 50 of the brighter members are visible to the naked eye. The cluster stands out extremely well in binoculars, but poorly in a telescope because the cluster is so large. The bulk of the stars lie with 5° but the outliers extend to a surprising 25°. In 50,000 years, the cluster will have moved to where Betelgeuse presently is and be so far away that it will appear as a small telescopic object. Light from the Hyades takes 130 years to reach us.

Only a fist diameter to the northwest of the Hyades is the next best naked-eye open cluster in the sky: *the Pleiades*. Most people observing from a fairly dark sky can see 7 stars but keen young eyes under perfect conditions can detect 9 and up to 12 of the cluster's brightest members. Binoculars or very small telescopes show it beautifully. Large apertures will faintly reveal the *Merope Reflection Nebula* extending south from the star Merope (the bright star towards the bottom in the photograph on page 82).

The fourth brightest open cluster is *Praesepe* or the *Beehive Cluster*, in *Cancer*. It looks like a small circular mist to the naked eye but in the smallest telescope it will resolve into at least a couple of dozen stars. Ancient peoples never knew what the '*Cloudy One*' was until Galileo invented the telescope in 1610 and exposed the mystery as a mass of glittering stars. Although there are only a few dozen bright members, when all the faint members are counted there is a total membership of about 350. The light we see today from the Beehive left its stars about 500 years ago.

NGC 3532
Carina

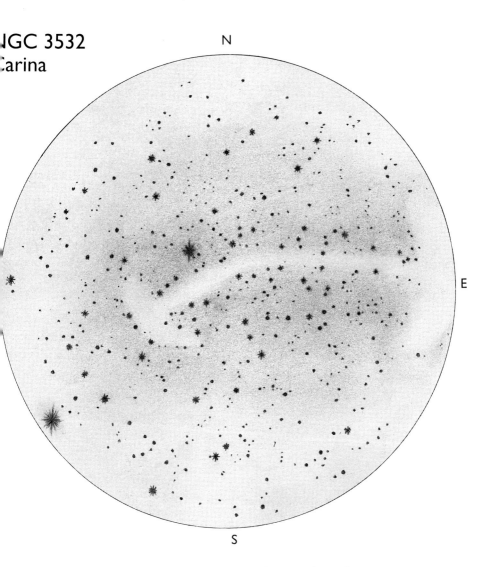

NGC 3532 is the sky's best telescopic galactic cluster. It lies a fist, at arm's length, west of the Southern Cross in the same low-powered field as the Eta Carinae Nebula. Its 200 fairly bright stars are 'split' by a strange narrow void with mushroom-shaped ends. A brilliant red star is on its outer edge and another less bright one lies near its centre. Drawing: GD Thompson

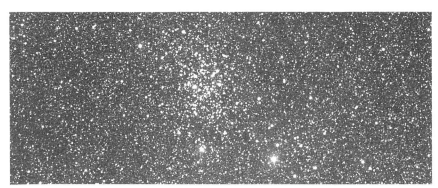

Drift along the southern Milky Way into the Norma star cloud and you will be treated to this bright, rich open cluster, NGC 6067, set against a dense background of faint Milky Way stars. Binoculars show nine red giants amongst a mass of bluish ones.

At the right-angle bend in the Scorpion's tail are two naked-eye double stars shown at left and right. Between them lies this wonderful region called the Zeta Scorpii Complex. This picture shows a binocular view portraying an emission nebula and a compact star cluster NGC 6321 to the right, together with dark nebulae across the field.

A magnified telescopic view of the delicate star cluster NGC 6231 beside the double star Zeta, which has red and blue components. Photos: S Quirk

M7 is a very obvious, comet-like, bright spot in the Milky Way near the Scorpion's Sting. It is well resolved in binoculars and its large ¹/₂° diameter needs low power. It has about 80 stars brighter than magnitude 10 and an orange star lies on its edge. The light we see from M7 left 800 years ago.

The Southern Pleiades is no match for its northern counterpart. Nevertheless, it is a beautiful cluster of around 20 stars, visible in binoculars, surrounding the star Theta Carinae. Keen-sighted observers will see about seven or eight stars with the naked eye. The remote cluster to the right of centre is Mel 101.

The Jewel Box is one of the finest telescopic clusters. It has an obvious A-shape of bright stars. The central bar members are red, blue and white 'jewels'. Masses of fainter stars gather around these supergiants. It is bright enough to be seen with the smallest of optical aids as a hazy spot on the eastern side of the second brightest star in the Southern Cross, Beta Crucis. Photos: S Quirk

CHAPTER THIRTEEN

HUNTING CELESTIAL SMOKE RINGS

When old stars become unstable (that is, once much of their fuel is burned), they are thought to expand and shed their outer layers in the form of a bubble-like shell of extremely rarefied gas called *Planetary Nebula*. The famous 18th-century English astronomer Sir William Herschel gave these objects their name because many small ones resembled the disc of Uranus as seen in telescopes of the day.

The gas expands until it completely dissipates. Such stars can lose their outer envelopes in a series of 'hiccups' over a long period, and therefore more than one shell can sometimes be seen. The central stars, which are often visible, excite the gas enough to fluoresce; the colours depend on the types of gases involved and the energy output of the central star.

There are about 100 planetaries that are within reach of amateur telescopes; however, when hunting them, be forewarned that many are so small at low power that they cannot be distinguished from other field stars. So it is important to take the time to find the right field at low power before changing to high power to detect the object. At high power, stars will remain points of light but the planetary will become an obvious disc — providing it is bright enough to be seen in your telescope. Many of the larger ones are typically very faint.

After you have gained some experience finding the larger and brighter planetaries, use a good telescopic star atlas to find *NGC 6572* in Ophiuchus. Observe how blue its bright circular disc is and then compare it to the green colour of *NGC 3918* in Vela, just west of the Southern Cross.

PLANETARIES

NGC 7293, the *Helix Nebula*, in Aquarius, is the largest of the planetaries within easy reach of small telescopes. In fact, its ¼° diameter can be glimpsed in binoculars. In a telescope it is faint, but a dark sky will reveal its smoke ring appearance. It is called the *Helix* because photographs taken with large telescopes display a double structure and explosive streaks can also be seen radiating from the faint central star. Because the Helix Nebula contains a lot of oxygen as well as hydrogen it glows very brightly with an OIII filter, making it visible even under full moonlight.

M27 (NGC 6853), the *Dumbbell Nebula*, is a favourite in the northern constellation of Vulpecula. Situated amongst rich Milky Way star clouds, M27 hangs like a 8 arc minutes by 5 arc minutes Dumbbell, with the outer edges being the brightest. An OIII filter changes its shape completely, making visible the normally faint, elongated, greenish haze lying perpendicular to the bright section. You can use lots of power on this bright nebula. The light we see from the Dumbbell has travelled across space for nearly 700 years to reach us.

M57 (NGC 6720), the *Ring Nebula*, lies low in the northern sky for the observers in the far southern states of Australia, but it is well worth hunting down. It lies between two 3rd magnitude stars half a fist south (above) the bright star Vega, in Lyra. The ring is most distinct, even in reasonably small telescopes at moderate powers. Because M57 is bright for such objects, it magnifies well. This planetary is about 5500 years old, half a lightyear across and about 2000 lightyears away.

NGC 3132, the *Eight-burst Nebula*, lies at -40° declination to the north of the *False Cross*. It is the southern sky's answer to the Ring Nebula in Lyra. They are both about the same size although 3132's central star is much brighter. It is estimated to be 2600 lightyears away. Large telescope photographs capture a magnificent series of rings that suggest that the central star has 'burst' eight times. Visually, in moderate-sized amateur telescopes, it displays an elongated C-shaped ring around the central star. Apertures 20cm and larger begin to show its blue-green colour.

NGC 7009, the *Saturn Nebula*, in Aquarius, is a must to observe. In amateur scopes at high power, it is bright, featuring a shape distinctly like an eye. Telescopes larger than 25cm will detect the faint thin extensions emanating from the long axis, which resemble the rings of Saturn seen nearly edge-on. The Saturn Nebula has a distinctly blue colour. In binoculars or viewfinders, it looks like an 8th magnitude star. The drawing was made at 780x with an OIII filter.

NGC 3242, the *Ghost of Jupiter Nebula*, on Hydra, is just over 20° almost due north of 3132. This planetary appears bluish even in moderate instruments. It has an eye-like bright centre about half a minute long by a quarter of a minute wide, surrounding its 11th magnitude central star. Outside this is a fainter envelope from an earlier outburst that is about twice the dimensions of the brighter inner section. It is about 2000 lightyears from us. The drawing was made at 660 times magnification under very good seeing.

NGC 246, the *Cetus Bubble*, is a large but fairly faint planetary with several faint stars involved. It is irregularly round and unevenly bright. An OIII filter and a power of 187 was employed to make the drawing.

NGC 5189, the *Spiral Planetary*, is a superbly detailed, strange planetary. Because it lies in the far southern constellation of Musca, it is relatively unknown. It is fairly bright and takes magnification well. Its 2 arc minutes diameter form stands out well against a beautiful Milky Way star field. The drawing was made at a magnification of 330.

NGC 1360, the *Comet Planetary*, looks identical to a tailless comet with a starlike nucleus. It lies in *Fornax* and was only recently identified as a planetary. Its large diameter of 7 arc minutes required a low power of only 66x to make the drawing. This planetary is estimated to be about 1000 lightyears away.

NGC 6752, the *Turquoise Orb*, is a small, bright orb of intensely turquoise light that fades away rapidly at the edges. It is slightly brighter towards the northwest side. The Turquoise Orb is the most richly coloured nebula for small telescopes.

To see colour and detail well in planetaries, apertures in excess of 20cm are required.

Opposite: These planetaries were drawn at the eyepiece using a 32cm reflector at high power with an OIII filter. Note the interesting diversity.
Drawing: GD Thompson

Planetary Nebulae

Nebula

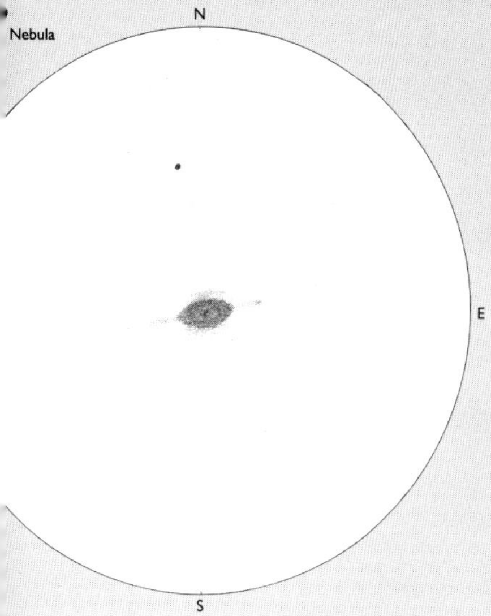

N

S

NGC 3242
The Ghost of Jupiter
(Hydra)

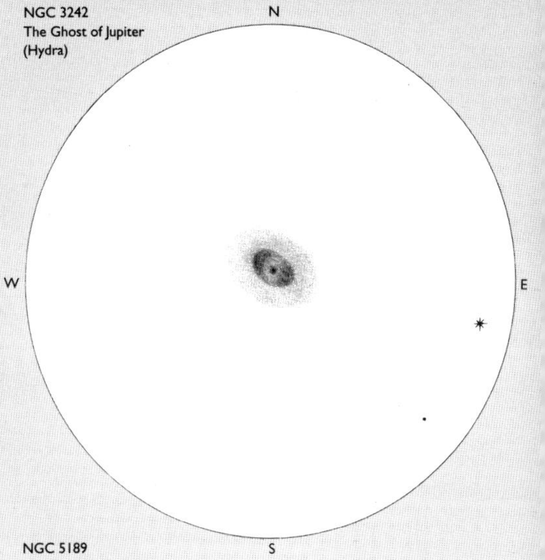

N

E W

E

S

Nebula

N

S

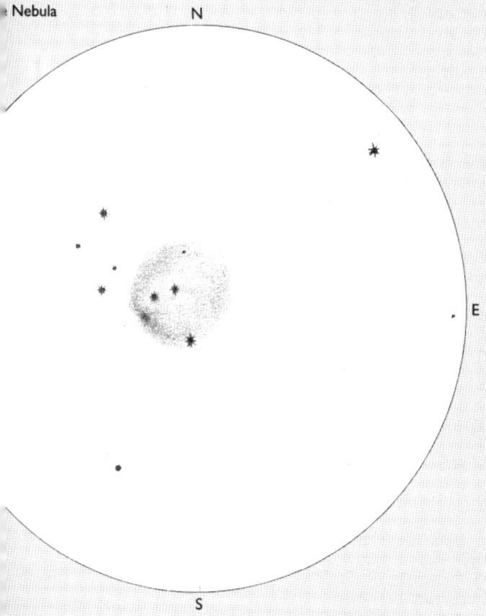

NGC 5189
The Spiral Planetary
(Musca)

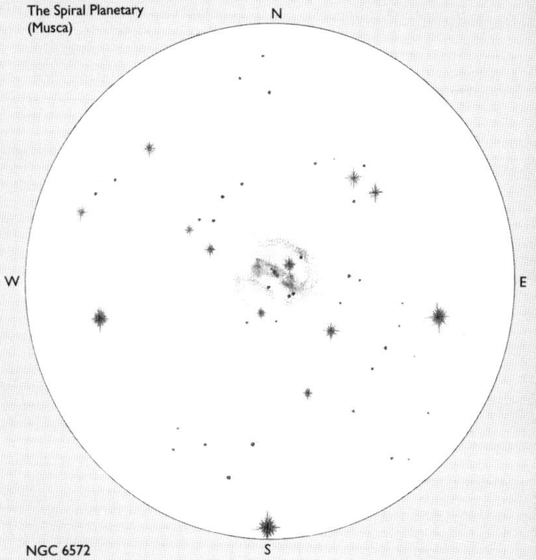

N

E W

E

S

Planetary

N

E W

E

S

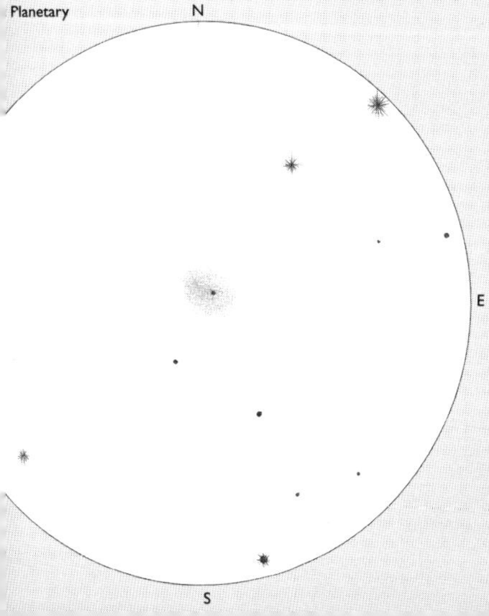

NGC 6572
The Turquoise Orb
(Orphuichus)

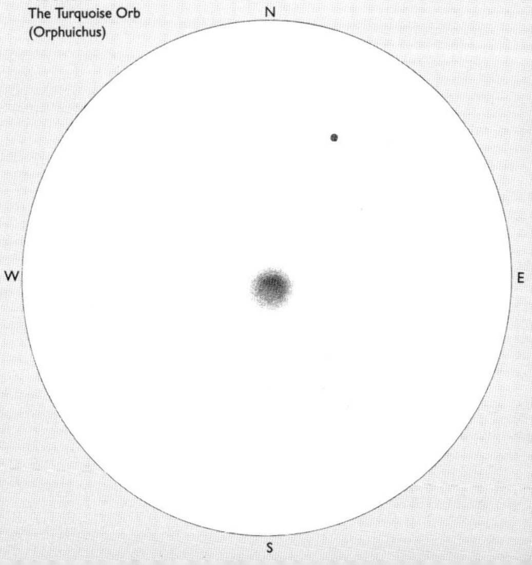

N

E

S

CHAPTER FOURTEEN

GLOBULARS — HEAVENLY SPHERES OF MILLIONS OF SUNS

No one fails to be astonished when they look at a bright, rich *Globular Cluster* in a dark sky through a 20cm, or larger, telescope. Globulars can contain hundreds of thousands of stars compacted together so tightly at the centre that it can appear solid.

Unlike Galactic Clusters, which reside in the spiral arms, about 200 globulars form a type of globular cluster themselves, clustering around the galaxy's nucleus and occupying a spherical space with a diameter about the size of the galaxy.

Globular star populations range from tens of thousands to over a million. They are like miniature spherical galaxies. Some astronomers believe that there may be large numbers of stray globulars in intergalactic space. The stars in globulars appear fainter than bright open clusters because they are so much further away, usually tens of thousands of lightyears compared to the hundreds of lightyears for most open clusters. A globular's myriad of suns move around the cluster's imaginary centre in huge elliptical orbits that take hundreds of thousands of years to complete. The stars in a globular's core seem to be touching, but they can be lightyears apart to maybe thousands per cubic lightyear.

Surprisingly, if we were located inside an average globular, the night sky might look fairly similar to ours except there would be a more even distribution of faint stars with a significant increase in the number of bright ones with many outshining Venus. The Milky Way would appear as a large elliptical haze in one part of the sky.

Few observers realise that each star they are seeing in a globular is either a giant or a group of bright stars appearing as one. The Milky Way's globulars are very old at 10 billion years, having formed at the same time as the galaxy.

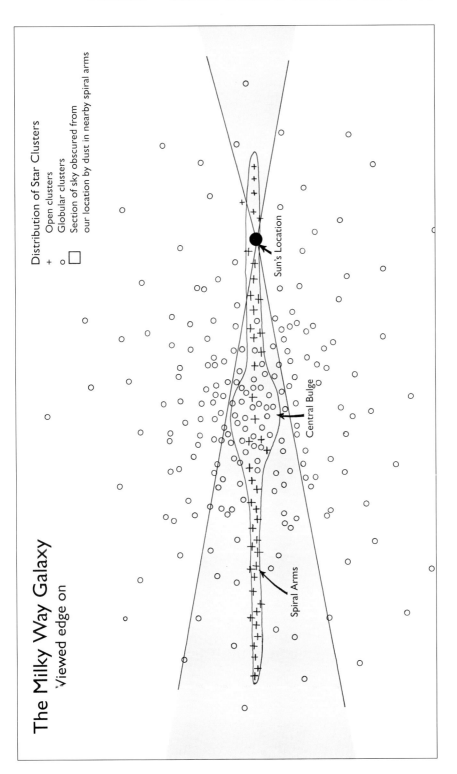

The Milky Way Galaxy
Viewed edge on

Distribution of Star Clusters

+ Open clusters
o Globular clusters
☐ Section of sky obscured from our location by dust in nearby spiral arms

Sun's Location

Central Bulge

Spiral Arms

Globular Clusters

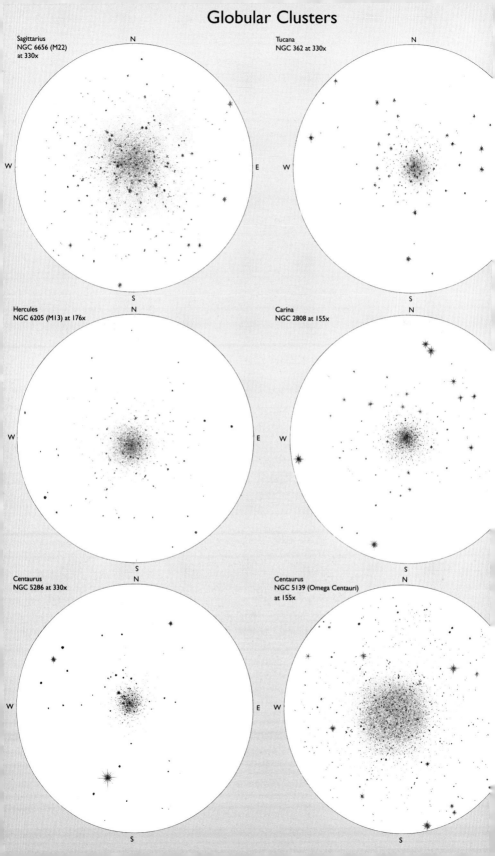

Sagittarius
NGC 6656 (M22)
at 330x

Tucana
NGC 362 at 330x

Hercules
NGC 6205 (M13) at 176x

Carina
NGC 2808 at 155x

Centaurus
NGC 5286 at 330x

Centaurus
NGC 5139 (Omega Centauri)
at 155x

From our viewpoint, at least one-third of our galaxy's globulars are hidden by the galaxy's spiral arms, while others are made extremely faint and reddened by interstellar dust. However, a few large ones that are relatively close to us are bright enough to be glimpsed with the naked eye, appearing as faint hazy stars. Of the six finest, all are southern objects. A few of the best are either faintly visible to the naked eye or plainly visible in binoculars.

Tucanae 47 or *NGC 104* competes with Omega Centauri for being the most spectacular globular in the heavens. It lies on the western edge of the Small Magellanic Cloud. It is estimated to contain at least half a million stars. There may also be many very faint stars that are yet undetected. A 10cm telescope will resolve Tuc 47's brightest members. The photons of light from Tuc 47's stars have been travelling to us unimpeded for 15,000 years.

The cluster is so large that it would take 200 years at the speed of light to cross it. Telescopically, Tuc 47 has a very bright, slightly yellowish core that appears like a globular itself sitting directly on top of a larger, somewhat bluish, background of cluster members. In the same photograph is another very distant globular 180,000 lightyears further away in another galaxy — the Small Magellanic Cloud. This globular is designated *NGC 121* and it appears as a bright hazy star on the right-hand side of the picture amongst Tuc 47's outliers. In a 32cm telescope at high power, it appears as a hazy orb. Coincidentally, at a similar distance on the other side of Tuc 47 (just outside the picture), lies another slightly larger and fainter SMC globular. This is the only region in the sky where three globulars appear to touch and lie in a straight line!

NGC 5139, Omega Centauri, is the largest and most massive globular visible. The light from these distant suns combine together to appear like a blurry 4th magnitude star to the naked eye. It has an even larger diameter than Tuc 47, having the same diameter as the Moon. Its noticeably elliptical form indicates the whole cluster is rotating relatively fast. Look for two oval patches just off centre that look like owl eyes. They are hidden in the photograph due to the bright core being overexposed. They are not dark globules projected against it but a chance alignment of bright and faint cluster members. Variable stars in Omega have permitted the distance to be measured at nearly 17,000 lightyears. Omega lies at the end of a line extended northeast through *Gamma* and *Delta Crucis* (the 3rd and 4th brightest stars of the Southern Cross) and four times their separation (12°).

Opposite: Many of the southern sky's most beautiful globulars are rich and bright and can be well resolved in amateur telescopes. These high accuracy drawings were made at the eyepiece by the author using a 32cm telescope at moderately high powers. Drawings: GD Thompson

The great, far southern globular, Tucanae 47, is spectacular in any telescope larger than 10cm. It is half a million suns compressed to a bright, dense core.

Omega Centauri, NGC 5139, is the largest of all known globular clusters, containing in excess of one million suns.

NGC 6397 has probably less than 100,000 stars. At low power its compacted core stars seem almost starlike. Photos: S Quirk

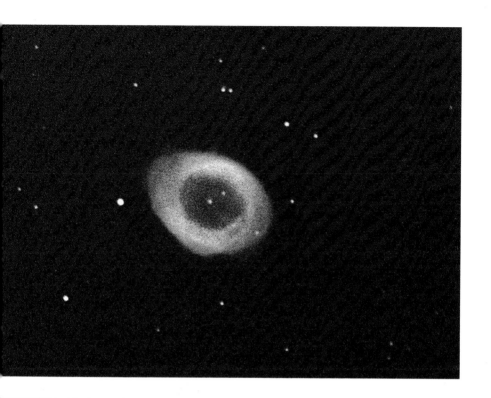

beautiful cosmic smoke rings that surround central stars. The Ring Nebula (M57) *ra (top) and the Eight Burst Nebula (NGC 3132) in Vela. Stars can become* *ible and expand to form such planetary nebulae.* M57 Photo J Marling, NGC 3132 Photo ESO

The Sombrero Galaxy's central hub is much larger than the Milky Way's and its dust lanes are so dense they can be seen in small telescopes. The faint blue stars surrounding it are M104's globular clusters. Photo European Southern Observatory (ESO), Chile

The Great Barred Spiral in Fornax (NGC 1365) is the best example of its kind in the sky. It shows considerable detail in large amateur telescopes. Photo ESO

Top to bottom: M4, M55, NGC 6752. These are some of the southern sky's most interesting globulars. Note the diversity in star populations and the degree of concentration. Photos: J Marling (top), S Quirk (others)

NGC 6397, in Ara, appears to be the closest of all globulars, at around 8000 lightyears. Its brightest members are red giants with luminosities about 500 times that of the Sun.

M4, NGC 6121, is situated only 1° due west of Antares. An interesting feature of M4 is that it has a bar of fairly bright, 11th magnitude stars across its centre. It is not as condensed as the aforementioned globulars.

M55, NGC 6809, is half the Moon's diameter in size and visible in binoculars about 8° due east of the *Teapot's* handle in Sagittarius. It is a rich, compact globular but it looks very open visually because most of the stars are too faint to see individually.

NGC 6752 can be found in Pavo at the same declination as *Beta Crucis*. It is bright in binoculars and well resolved in moderate-sized telescopes. This globular is the 3rd largest in the sky. It is estimated to be about 20,000 lightyears away.

M22, NGC 6656 is a spectacular and very rich cluster that outshines the famous Hercules Cluster, M13, the best in the northern sky. It is visible to the naked eye and a 20cm telescope begins to show resolution. In a 30cm reflector at moderate power, its half a million stars are a breathtaking sight. When we look at M22, we are looking at it as it was about 22,000 years ago.

NGC 362 lies just off the northern edge of the Small Magellanic Cloud. It is easily detected in binoculars, and at high power in a 32cm telescope it can be mistaken for Tuc 47. Because NGC 362 is so close to Tuc 47, this excellent cluster is often overshadowed.

M13, NGC 6205, the *Great Hercules Cluster*, is well viewed from the northern half of Australia but appears low in the sky for far southern observers. Together with two faint stars flanking it, M13 is just barely visible to the naked eye. It is a fine globular in a large aperture scope, being well resolved into numerous stars. M13 seems to have a population as large as Omega, but it is further away at 25,000 lightyears and consequently is less impressive.

NGC 2808, in Carina, halfway from the False Cross to Beta Carinae, is a lovely, bright, rich globular that is peppered with sparkling stardust.

NGC 5286 is a high surface brightness globular that lies beside the star M Centaurus.

Chapter Fifteen

Extragalactic Whirlpools across the Gulfs of Time

In the early part of this century, our galaxy was thought to be the entire universe. Distant galaxies were thought to be whirlpools of gas in *our* galaxy and, hence, they were called nebulae. Some astronomers suspected otherwise and, in the 1940s, using the Mt Wilson 100 inch telescope, then the world's largest, as well as newly developed films, they resolved the Andromeda Galaxy into extremely distant stars proving that these whirlpool-like nebulae were, themselves, galaxies in their own right, like the Milky Way, but very far away. This single discovery instantaneously made our universe billions of times larger.

When we leave our Milky Way Galaxy, we travel for nearly 200,000 lightyears until we pass the Magellanic Clouds; two satellite galaxies in orbit about our rather large spiral. It is another two and a quarter million lightyears before we encounter the *Great Andromeda Galaxy, M31*, which is half as large again as ours. The *Pinwheel Galaxy, M33*, in Triangulum, situated relatively close to M31, is about three million lightyears from us and it is about a third of the mass of the Milky Way.

Clustered around Andromeda, the Milky Way and M33, are more than 20 *Dwarf Elliptical* and *Dwarf Irregular* galaxies which contain only tens of millions to a few billion stars; much less than our own galaxy. Dwarfs are probably the most abundant types of galaxies in the universe but, because they are so faint, we can only see those nearby.

Once we leave the neighbourhood of these three spirals and their accompanying dwarfs, called the *Local Group*, we travel for approximately eight million lightyears to the *Sculptor Group*, which contains primarily *NGC 253, NGC 55, NGC 247, NCG 300* and *NGC 7793*. At 15 million lightyears, we reach another southern cluster of galaxies in the constellation of Centaurus, which includes *M83, NGC 5128, NGC 4945, NGC 5102* and

NGC 5068. Another 60 million lightyears brings us to the giant *Virgo Cluster* of galaxies in the northern sky. These galaxies are well observed from Australia, but the more compact and distant *Fornax Cluster* is too far south for most northern hemisphere observers to see well.

The Virgo Cluster forms the centre of the *Local Supercluster* (of galaxy clusters). There are innumerable clusters of galaxies strewn through filamentary chains that make up the superclusters. Recently, it was discovered that the superclusters themselves form a froth-like structure throughout the universe with huge voids of virtually nothing between the superclusters.

With the naked eye, we can see both Magellanic Clouds and M31 easily, but M33 is only glimpsed with difficulty. Binoculars show all four very well, in addition to scores of other galaxies seen as faint hazy objects. While the southern sky does not have a concentration of galaxies such as those in the Virgo Cluster, it has an unequalled display of large, bright galaxies of nearly every class. (The closest galaxies in the sky, the Magellanic Clouds, are discussed in the following chapter, devoted specially to them due to the extraordinary detail they present.)

Now, before we turn our telescopes into extragalactic space and observe some classic southern examples, a word of advice. You will need to make good use of dark adaption, averted vision and magnification. And be sure to observe under dark, moonless skies if you want to see galaxies at their best.

NGC 5236, M83, is a splendid spiral galaxy in Hydra. Photo: J Marling

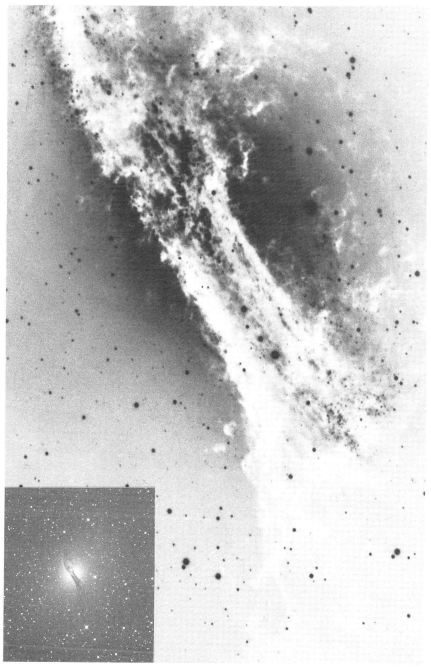

NGC 5128, Centaurus A, is a spectacular but peculiar southern galaxy possessing a massive dust lane that dissects this almost round elliptical. Perhaps a smaller galaxy has merged with the nucleus of what was once a normal spiral. Photo: AAT, inset photo: S Quirk

NGC 5128, Centaurus A, roars in a radio telescope due to the strong radio emission probably originating from a huge black hole in its nucleus. It is a peculiar galaxy, having a huge thick, disturbed dust lane crossing the bright cental core and almost totally obscuring it. NGC 5128 appears round like an EO type elliptical galaxy, but ellipticals are not supposed to have dust lanes. Astronomers cannot yet make sense of this anomaly. This galaxy lies 4° due north of Omega Centauri and it can be seen in binoculars as a tiny, faint glow. The dust lane is visible in any moderate aperture. The inset photograph, taken with a 25cm telescope, gives a good indication of its visual appearance in a moderate aperture at low power. The bright star in the dust lane near centre is no longer there: it was a supernova. Starlight from 5128 has taken 17 million years to reach us.

NGC 253, the *Silver Coin Galaxy*, is only slightly inclined from an edge-on view. It is about three-quarters the size of the Milky Way, lying at a distance of 10 million lightyears. Anglo-Australian Telescope photographs resolve numerous HII regions and star clusters. The spectacularly detailed photograph was taken with a 32cm telescope, and it shows two arms spiralling out from a small, bright nucleus. Even in 60mm telescopes, 253 shows its nearly ½° long oval form well. It is 7° south of Beta Ceti. Be sure not to mistake 253 for the globular *NGC 288*, 2° southeast of it.

NGC 253, the Silver Coin Galaxy, is the best telescopic galaxy in the sky.
Photo: M Spencer

The Spanish Dancer galaxy is a delicate, classic two-armed spiral. Photo: S Quirk

NGC 5236, M83, is a gem. It is a face-on spiral on the border of the constellation Hydra, nearly directly north of 5128. M83 is a barred spiral, similar in size to the Milky Way, and can be seen in a small telescope viewfinder. The nucleus is very bright and a 30cm telescope begins to resolve its spiral arms. For reasons unknown, this galaxy is a prodigious producer of supernovae having exhibited five such events in 60 years.

An Australian amateur astronomer, Robert Evans discovered a supernova in M83 as well as NGC 5128 (and many other galaxies), which has helped in determining distances to these galaxies.

The author and James Bryan Jr have produced a set of 236 charts together with a handbook on searching for supernovae, entitled the *Supernova Search Charts*. These detailed maps of the 300 brightest galaxies can be an asset to deep sky observers wishing to ferret out galactic detail and, of course, for writing your name in the stars by making a supernova discovery.

NGC 55, the *Cigar Galaxy,* is superbly detailed. Most galaxies are too distant to display much internal detail, but 55 does. Its ½° length is mottled with several large HII regions and stellar associations (large star clouds). These are easily visible in a 20cm scope. It is noticeably uneven in both brightness and width.

The *Fornax Cluster* contains around 20 galaxies, most within only 3° of sky. Because they are at a distance of 60 million lightyears, don't expect them to be large and bright. *NGC 1365,* the *Great Barred Spiral,* in Fornax,

The Great Centaurus Edgewise Spiral is obvious in binoculars, appearing as a slender oval of mist. Photo: S Quirk

is the largest member. A 20cm telescope will reveal the two spiral arms of this extraordinary giant. Its dust lane can be seen to almost intersect the nucleus in a 30cm aperture. Views in a 46cm reflector are unforgettable.

NGC 4594, M104, the *Sombrero Galaxy,* looks like a perfect celestial creation. The Sombrero features a huge central hub with an intensely bright core surrounded by spiral arms and dark dust lanes seen nearly edge-on. It lies a few degrees northeast of Corvus and is visible in binoculars at the end of a chain of stars. Even small telescopes show M104's spindle shape; however, in larger instruments at high power the dust lanes become obvious and it looks like a photograph.

NGC 4945, the *Great Centaurus Edgewise Spiral,* lies near a couple of 4th magnitude stars (Centaurus Xi¹ and Xi²) shown in the photograph. They are 8° northeast of the Southern Cross. NGC 4945 is a large slender ellipse 15 arc minutes x 2 arc minutes which is visible in binoculars, yet because of its far southern declination, it is not well known. It too is an edge-on spiral with very heavy, dark dust lanes — one obscures a noticeable portion of the northern end. To the left just outside the photo's edge is its neighbouring elliptical galaxy *NGC 4976.*

NGC 1566, the *Spanish Dancer Galaxy,* in Dorado, is a small but fairly bright, beautiful two-armed spiral. The arms can be resolved in a 30cm scope. Note that the large, faint outer arms which appear in the photograph are too faint to be seen with the eye.

CHAPTER SIXTEEN

THE SOUTHERN SKY'S BEST KEPT SECRET — THE MAGELLANIC CLOUDS

When Magellan sailed around the tip of South America in 1520, his sailors noticed two large detached portions of the Milky Way in the far southern sky only 20° from the South Celestial Pole. They had no idea what they were. They named them the *Clouds of Magellan*. Because the Clouds lie so far south, we who live in the southern hemisphere have a privileged view of the most spectacular galaxies in the sky.

(The Australian Aborigines had Dreamtime legends about The Clouds. As the story goes, a young Aboriginal boy and a young girl were in love, against the tribe's social rules and, unfortunately for them, they were both betrothed to others. When their secret love affair was discovered, they were both banished forever from the face of the Earth by the Dreamtime Spirits as a lesson to others to never do the same. They were thrown upward through the starry night sky immediately after their conduct was discovered. As the boy went through the celestial sphere he left, for all to see for all time, a hole in the sky, the Large Magellanic Cloud. His lover formed the Small Magellanic Cloud.)

The Large Magellanic Cloud (LMC) is an average-sized, Barred Spiral with a mass about one-twentieth that of the Milky Way. It appears somewhat distorted through the gravitational attraction of the Milky Way as it orbits our galaxy. The Small Magellanic Cloud (SMC) is an Irregular Galaxy. It is another 10,000 lightyears further away than the LMC and about half the mass.

The brightest portion of the LMC forms an L-shape with large, faint spiral arms curling back from each end. The SMC looks teardrop-shaped, and it is a little fainter and smaller that the LMC.

The clouds are the richest area of sky in the entire heavens. Both galaxies are a treasure trove of objects, having together nearly as many objects to look at as we can see in the entire Milky Way. I have made detailed observations of some 400 individual objects in both Clouds. There are so many fine objects to see, so let's look at some of the most obvious. Incidentally, an OIII filter and high powers of magnification will enormously improve the visibility of many of the gaseous emission nebulae in these galaxies.

NGC 2070, 30 Doradus, the *Tarantula Nebula*, is a sight to behold. Even though it lies in another galaxy, this extraordinary gaseous nebula can be seen with the naked eye! It appears as a hazy spot in the foot of the 'L'. Binoculars reveal its nebulous character and telescopes display a huge spider-like nebulosity surrounded by several other nebulae and star clusters that are also fascinating. The Tarantula has a mass calculated to be an incredible five million times the mass of the Sun, and a diameter of 800 lightyears. Lying inside its bright nucleus is a mysterious, supermassive object named R136. It is only half a lightyear across yet it has a mass thousands of times of the Sun. The Tarantula is so large and bright that if it replaced the Great Nebula in Orion, it would cast shadows and cover the entire constellation.

NGC 1763–69, the *LMC Lagoon,* is the second brightest object in the LMC. It can just be glimpsed with a keen naked eye under perfect conditions. In binoculars it is quite obvious, appearing as one object when, in fact, it is a tight group of several gaseous nebulae with sizeable star clusters centrally involved that have formed out of the gas. Note that the solar wind pressure from the stars has cleared the gas from their immediate neighbourhood of the cluster. The largest nebula of the group is twice the size of M8.

The western portion of the *LMC Bar* is a treasure of all sorts of objects: globulars, complex HII emission nebulae, large open star clusters and many, almost starlike, OIII nebulosities. In the photograph on page 110, note the massive globulars scattered throughout. The LMC has extremely populous open clusters that are associated with large HII regions. To be well viewed, the whole area needs slow inspection of each object.

The SMC contains its brightest objects in its "tail". A couple of the brightest pictured on page 108 can be detected in a dark sky using binoculars. In the main body of the SMC lies nearly a score of fairly faint HII regions which are greatly enhanced by the use of either an OIII or UHC filter. These are actually quite large to be seen so readily at such a distance. A wide field eyepiece will reveal up to fifteen! Observers with telescopes of 20cm or larger can search the opposite side of the SMC to Tuc 47 for a delicate chain of small star clusters and nebulosity.

In this wide-angle naked-eye view, we see the Clouds of Magellan as they appear in a dark sky. The Small Magellanic Cloud (SMC) is to the left with Tuc 47 appearing like a bright star at the far left. The central bar of the Large Magellanic Cloud (LMC) is evident with the Tarantula Nebula appearing as a spot at the top right. Photo: A Fujii

Above: NGC 1763–69, the LMC Lagoon, is a rich complex of objects, second in brightness only to the Tarantula Nebula. It is often overlooked because it lies alone on the outer northern edge of the galaxy. Photo: S Quirk

Opposite top: The Small Magellanic Cloud is a galaxy of billions of suns in orbit about the Milky Way. This picture simulates a large binocular view. Some of its most prominent objects are situated in the 'tip'. The globular clusters Tuc 47 and NGC 362 that belong to the Milky Way, are at right and far top, respectively. An OIII filter exposes over a dozen nebulae in the main body of the SMC. An outlying chain of SMC star clusters and nebulosity are faintly visible to the far left of the galaxy. Photo: S Quirk

Opposite bottom: A detailed view of NGC 371, NGC 346 and NGC 330 in the tip of the Small Magellanic Cloud. The brightest object NGC 346 (centre) is a huge Eta Carinae-sized nebula with an S-shape. The large cluster to the left (west) is NGC 371. An OIII filter reveals a nearly perfectly round disc of gas around this cluster. NGC 330 is the bright, very compact, hemispherical galactic cluster towards the bottom right. Photo: S Quirk

LMC northern spiral arm objects lie north of the Tarantula Nebula. This area is marvellous when using an OIII filter, especially with apertures larger than 20cm. At high power each object can be studied individually.

The LMC bar is filled with rich globular and open clusters as well as some large areas of faint nebulosity. Photo: S Quirk

CHAPTER SEVENTEEN

CONCEPTS OF SPACE AND TIME

When I have people observing with me in the field or at the observatory, there is usually a keen element who love discussing all the latest cosmological theories well into the night. This chapter is for all the armchair cosmologists who take pleasure in pondering the mysteries of the cosmos.

Time Viewing: When we look up at the night sky we are looking back in time. When we see the Sun, we see it as it was eight minutes ago or Saturn as it was over an hour ago. Because the distances are so great, it takes light that long to get to us. The deeper we look into space, the further back in time we see. For instance, Sirius is nine years old. When we look at the Magellanic Clouds, we are looking 170,000 years back in time and when we observe the most distant galaxies that our amateur telescopes will detect, we are seeing them as they were hundreds of million of years ago. The world's largest telescopes can see quasars and very bright galactic nuclei at the edge of the observable universe. Their light left on its journey towards us some billions of years ago — before our Solar System ever existed. We see things as they *were*; not as they are.

Einstein's Relativity — What Does it Really Mean? Several proofs of Einstein's Theory of Relativity have shown that the rate at which time passes is not constant. It will slow to a complete stop at the speed of light (*c*) or in an infinite gravitational field such as that of a black hole.

If we could observe with a super powerful telescope an imaginary, massless spaceship accelerating away from us, continuously getting faster and faster until it reached *c*, we would be able to watch the clocks (and the people) on board the spaceship appearing to go slower and slower until they completely stopped once they reached *c*.

To us it would appear as if the crew are frozen in time. Time dilation effects are so dramatic near *c* that, to the crew, even after travelling for billions of earth years, it would appear, to them, as if it were only a short trip to the other side of the universe! The only way the crew would be aware that anything had changed would be to look at the view outside. As they accelerate, the stars directly in front become bluer and then more violet until they become so ultraviolet that they cannot be seen at all. The stars behind would become redder and redder until they faded away into infrared heat. If it were possible to approach the speed of light, an amazing thing would occur: the stars *behind* the ship would appear to be crowded onto the *forward* viewscreen in a tunnel vision appearance. Those directly in front would appear blue. As they move outwards, they become red, only to fade into darkness as they move towards the outside of the viewscreen.

If they observed us, it would appear to them as if *we* are accelerating away from them, so they see us slowing down. The information flowing between Earth and the spaceship via light is taking longer and longer as the ship continues to accelerate and increase the distance between them.

Einstein's theory also demonstrated that, as things move faster, they become shorter and shorter in the direction that they are travelling, until, at c, they have no length at all! That is, to an observer watching from the sidelines. Anyone on the spaceship would think nothing had changed length because their rulers would also shrink. Contrary to our earthly experience, both length and time are elastic if our velocity or gravitational field changes significantly.

Time Travel: To travel at the speed of light is impossible in reality because to accelerate even the tiniest particle to c requires infinite energy. Any mass will increase more and more as it accelerates to become infinite at c.

If we could travel not at the speed of light but a little below it (at relativistic speeds) where time dilation effects are still appreciable, then we could, theoretically, visit another star system 200 lightyears away. We would take, say, a year to travel there, then another to study it and another to return. We would only be three years older, but 403 earth years could have gone by on Earth during our absence! We would effectively be propelled into the future.

Exceeding the Universal Speed Limit: By utilising today's advanced Virtual Reality computer technology we are already learning how to create extremely realistic imaginary worlds to bring the universe to us rather than attempting to travel to it. The more accurately we describe the universe with our sciences using sophisticated mathematics, the more real our simulated worlds become and the more sensors we can use to explore them. In them, we can travel faster than light and we can never die but we can experience them as if we were there, just as an airline pilot does in a simulator.

C 300, The Southern Pinwheel Galaxy, appears like a half sized 'duplicate' of its ⁊ern namesake. The red line is a satellite trail. Photo European Southern Observatory (ESO) Chile

Cigar Galaxy (NGC 55) is one of the most splendid galaxies in the sky that can be ⁊ved with a small telescope. Note the internal detail. Photo ESO

The Large Magellanic Cloud as seen through binoculars. Both NGC 2070 (bright sp○ at top) and the NGC 1763-69 group (lower right) are faintly visible even to the nak○ eye. Note the central bar and its disrupted arms. Photo R Royer

*The spidery 'legs' of the Tarantula Nebula blaze in a telescope, even though its light has travelled across space for 170,000 years to reach us. It is the largest **known** gaseou○ nebula in the universe. Note the profusion of other objects around it.* Photo S Quirk

Participating in the Past: It is theoretically possible to travel into the future but never into the past. If we *were* capable of travelling faster than light to perhaps go *backwards* in time, then some impossible things could happen. For example, we could go back into the past and accidentally, unknowingly or otherwise kill ourselves or our ancestors. If that happened, we would never exist in the future to be able to go back into the past in the first place. To physically change anything in the past would create a 'tidal wave' of infinite chain reactions. Time travel to the past can be proven to be impossible no matter how advanced our technology may become. We may view the past with great precision in the future but we will never participate in it.

The Effect of Chaos: The Chaos Theory demonstrates that the most infinitesimal change in any system can multiply until it affects the stability or outcome of larger and larger systems, including the universe itself. Chaos will make the planets ultimately fly away into space. Although chaos appears to be unpredictable, science has discovered that there is order within chaos. Chaos appears to be built in to the rules of the universe to create constant change and evolution. Life appears to be anti-chaotic: designed to organise and counter the apparent disorder chaos creates.

Photon Ride: Photons are light particles (or energy packages) which have no mass, so they are permitted to travel at c. Imagine riding on a photon, the universe would have no dimensions at all! At c, all distances and time shrink to zero and therefore do not exist. We could be at every point in the universe at the same time because it would take no time to travel no distance!

Black Holes and Neutron Stars: Relativity also stated that the greater the gravitational field, the slower time would tick. Our Sun has a greater mass than the Earth and therefore a greater gravitational field than the Earth, so time ticks slightly slower on the Sun. When neutron stars are formed after a supernova implosion of a large star's core, the pressures reached in the collapse are incredible. Under such extreme pressures, negatively charged electrons, which do not like getting too close to positively charged protons (the nuclei of atoms), are forced to combine with protons, forming neutrally charged neutrons. All the space between the particles previously held apart by the electromagnetic force can now become filled with neutrons. Space that was previously filled with only a few atomic particles now accommodates trillions. It is no wonder a star millions of kilometres across collapses to only a few. And it is no surprise that the neutron star's surface gravity increases enormously. A neutron star having the mass of the Earth would only be about a kilometre across. If the mass and pressures are great enough, then it is thought that the star's core will collapse all the way into a black hole. For Earth to become a black hole it would have to be compressed to 2mm.

All matter falls inexorably into oblivion once it passes through the 'time gate' of a black hole's event horizon (black sphere at centre). As the matter spirals inwards in the accretion disc, it radiates much of its energy. Black holes are thought to abound throughout the universe; some being as massive as entire galaxies while others may be microscopic in size. It is theorised that infinite numbers of other universes may be continuously being born into other dimensions from existing black holes in our universe and, indeed, ours may have originated from another black hole itself.

Gravity Hollows: Einstein also calculated that gravity fields distort space. A simple way to explain this is to imagine a trampoline's mat representing any plane in space. Now let's place a ball bearing on the trampoline and note that it makes a small indentation in the mat's surface. This might represent Earth. If we take a bowling ball and place it on the mat, the depression is much greater. This could represent the Sun. If you roll a marble across the mat it will not travel in a straight line now that the balls have distorted 'space'. The marble will roll down into the 'Sun's gravity hollow', around the bowling ball and most probably back towards you if it travels close to the 'Sun'. This is what sun-grazing comets do.

The planets are always trying to 'roll down' into the Sun's gravity hollow. They don't succeed because there is very little friction in space, so they just keep orbiting for billions of years. If the marble didn't lose its energy through friction with the mat, it would keep orbiting the bowling ball forever too. Keep in mind that this distortion of space in the presence of matter happens in *every* plane, unlike the trampoline mat which only has one plane.

To demonstrate a black hole's gravity hollow, we have to imagine the mat has unlimited elasticity. To simulate a black hole, imagine placing a super, super-dense pinhead that weighs more than several mountain ranges on the centre of the mat. The mat's centre keeps stretching down, forming a bottomless pit.

A black hole's 'gravity well' can swallow huge numbers of stars that come too close and in the process becomes more massive and increases its gravitational attraction to attract more still! The matter just disappears out of the dimensions we experience, but the effects of the mass are still felt. It is a little like some two-dimensional beings who live on a 2D (flat) sheet of paper. They only know of the dimensions of width and breadth and are not aware of the third dimension of height. We drop a ruler across their world and it completely divides it in two. To them, the ruler is just a line. They have no idea where it came from nor do they know where it went when we picked it up.

Escape Velocity: To escape the gravity of a small asteroid, all you would need to do is jump like Superman. To escape Earth's gravity, we need our powerful rockets to exceed 40,000km/h. To climb up out of the Sun's gravity hollow to travel to another star, we must exceed 70,000km/h. The gravity well of a black hole is so 'vertical' that it cannot be climbed. One would need to travel faster than c, which is impossible; so everything that goes in, remains there.

A black hole has no size: it is infinitely smaller than an electron! Incredibly, though, it may have the mass of millions of suns. The *point* through which all matter disappears is called the *singularity*. Around the singularity is volume of space that appears as a black sphere called the *event horizon*. Inside the event horizon, the escape velocity is at least c so not even light can escape. Outside it, the escape velocity falls below c.

If matter can be attracted to the black hole from a nearby star, then it will spiral in towards the hole forming an *accretion disc*. Matter in the accretion disc releases great amounts of energy as it is crushed into sub-atomic particles. This is what we believe we are observing when we see *Quasars*. Gigantic black holes are believed to exist at the centres of many galaxies.

The Expansion of the Universe: Hubble discovered that the more distant a galaxy is, the faster it appeared to be receding from us. This has been interpreted as the expansion of the universe. As galaxies get further and further away, their recessional velocity increases until they approach the speed of light. They become increasingly redder and duller, ultimately becoming invisible at the edge of the *observable* universe. That is, although the universe may extend for finite or infinite distances beyond the edge of the observable universe, we can only ever see a spherical portion of the whole universe from any one location.

If we have interpreted the expansion of the universe correctly, then this implies a beginning and an end. This led to the *Big Bang Theory*. The theory predicts that the universe explodes from a singularity, to expand forever or, alternatively, if there is enough matter in the universe, it will slow to a halt and contract back into another singularity, perhaps to repeat the process again. Nature continually demonstrates that the more we learn, the more complex things become. The Big Bang seems too simplistic. The new *Plasma Theory* explains the structure of the universe as being due to the forces of electricity and magnetism *as well as* gravity. It fits observation well and overcomes some of the Big Bang's dilemmas.

The Edge of the Universe: The infinite size of the universe can be likened to the Earth's surface being unbounded and therefore infinite. Whilst Earth's surface area is finite, we could draw the straight line across the surface forever. The edge of the observable universe can be likened to standing on the Earth's surface and only being able to see to the horizon even though the surface extends far beyond.

Just as the concept of the Earth being round was so difficult for people of past eras to conceive even though the evidence was all around them, many of our present cosmological concepts are surely conceptually limited as well.

CHAPTER EIGHTEEN

PRESERVING THE NIGHT'S NATURAL BEAUTY

Many of us are taught as children to seek security in light at night and to unquestioningly fear the dark. This obsession with the need for light, combined with the need for power utilities to sell electricity, has helped to fuel an explosion of waste energy in the form of obtrusive outdoor lighting that is polluting our planet and stealing the night from us.

Over the last 25 years, the night sky has brightened dramatically in populated areas and it is predicted to become 50 times brighter still in the next 20 years!

This is happening because many outdoor lights in use today are left on when not needed. Others, such as floodlights on building and signs, are directed skywards. Many lights are very poorly designed, permitting large percentages of their light to be wasted by permitting it to radiate far beyond where it is needed.

Such wasted light causes numerous problems. For astronomers, it causes the night sky to become so bright around populated areas that only the brightest stars are easily visible. In most of Europe and North America, Urban Sky Glow has become so severe that there is almost nowhere left to go to see a naturally dark sky. In Australia, a similar deterioration is occurring, especially along the eastern seaboard and around all developed areas. Even the Yulara Resort, at Ayers Rock, that advertises the night sky as its third natural wonder, is unnecessarily light polluted from unshielded lights.

Simple, inexpensive shields on many lights will reduce sky glow. In many cases, the lights can simply be turned off after a particular time when they are no longer needed. One of the worst polluters of the night are security lights that don't need to be left on all night. They can have inexpensive motion activation sensors fitted so that the light only turns on when it senses human movement; most effective deterrent against intruders. Also, having a

Because so much light is wasted and directed needlessly into the sky, instead of seeing stars we see urban sky glow. Simple solutions mentioned in this chapter can help solve this problem and save the night. Photo: GD Thompson

light turning on and off attracts attention. Having the light off when it is not needed saves energy and the night sky.

The notion that light creates security is a false one. Security lights that stay on all night make the work of a thief or an assailant so much easier. So-called 'security' lighting actually assists criminals. For example, lighting helps them to see if a watchdog is around and whether there is anything worth stealing. Lights make it much easier to study their victim's movements and to know where access is best. Under a spotlight, ourselves and our property become sitting targets. It is understandable that many businesses and residences are often burgled and vandalised immediately after 'security lights' are installed. If, however, motion-activated lighting is installed then security is truly enhanced. Such lights come on when activated by the movement of a human body. They take an intruder by surprise and their flashing attracts attention. They cost little yet provide nearly 100% saving on electricity costs. It makes so much sense to have effective security at almost no cost and no pollution of the environment.

Another way to reduce light pollution is to have architectural and billboard lights lit from above rather than below, and they, too, should have a curfew (say, 10.30pm). Many lights have a much brighter bulb than is

Less than 40 years ago the sky looked like this picture even from the inner suburbs of most Australian cities. Sensible outdoor lighting could stop us losing this awesome beauty forever. Photo: R McNaught

required, so changing it for a lower wattage one will reduce glare, wastage and the consumer's electricity bill.

Not only astronomers are affected by light pollution. Obtrusive light around airports, railway stations, and shipping channels is making it difficult to see airstrip landing lights, signals and beacons, especially in bad weather. Authorities warn that it is likely to cause a major accident sooner or later if not addressed. Motorists are blinded or confused, especially in wet weather, by glaring lights that increase the likelihood of accidents. So it is important not to have fittings that radiate light indiscriminately.

Scientists are becoming aware of increasingly large numbers of nocturnal animals that are also adversely affected by not having a naturally dark night. For example, turtles crawl towards beach resort lights instead of the light of the Moon over the ocean. Night-flying birds that navigate by the stars become disorientated by brilliant lights on city buildings. Numerous species of insects, such as fireflies and moths, cannot compete with, or are confused by, man-made lights and, consequently, they are becoming extinct or threatened. There are numerous species of flora that cannot survive having their day–night cycle upset by lights that burn through the night.

We should never forget that every time we waste light we must burn more coal to produce the electricity. A massive 50% of all carbon dioxide gas emissions in Australia that pollute our air and cause the Greenhouse Effect are from our coal-burning power stations. And to think our methods of producing energy and light are so inefficient that only about 3% of the coal's energy gets converted to light. To make it even worse, we generally waste more than half the light we produce!

The light domes we see over our cities from a distance is waste light radiating into outer space where no one can use it. We all pay for that waste, so we should all do our share not to pollute our night. It can be worth discussing your environmental concerns and the solutions suggested with your local council member and your state and federal government representatives.

We all need light, in the right area, at the right time, but we must be aware not to contribute to a costly, wasteful and inconsiderate use of it or the romance of the night will be lost forever. If we practice less waste ourselves and educate others about the aforementioned solutions, we may be able to retain enough of the natural night so that we won't have to drive for days to a desert to stargaze under a naturally dark sky. Our descendants also might be able to witness the awesome beauty of the starry heavens.

GLOSSARY

ASTRONOMY: The science of understanding the workings of the universe.

ARC MINUTES: A measure of angular distance between two points.

BIG BANG THEORY: A cosmological model that attempts to explain the origin of the universe as being created in an enormous explosion which expanded from a single point to its present structure over approximately the last 15 billion years.

BLACK HOLE: An infinitely dense object. Gravity has compressed it so much that it occupies no space at all. The effects of its mass gravely distort space and time around it.

BOLIDE: An extremely bright meteor, also called a fireball.

CONSTELLATION: A region of sky. Most of the 88 constellations contain stars that vaguely represent forms derived from ancient folklore.

COMA 1: The huge, highly rarefied gaseous envelope that surrounds the nucleus of a comet.

COMA 2: A flaring imaging defect in an optical system.

ELLIPSE: An oval form that is not strictly circular, eg. the orbits of the planets, comets and asteroids.

GALAXY: A large assemblage of billions of stars that form into spiral, spherical or elliptical shapes.

GLOBULAR: Spherical cluster of hundreds of thousands of stars. Globular clusters surround galaxies.

GRAVITY LENSES: A lensing effect caused by gravity. Light from distant objects can be bent when it passes close to a strong gravitational field.

LIGHTYEAR: The distance light travels in one year — approximately 9,500,000,000,000 kms.

LIMB: The edge of a body eg. sun, moon, planet or star.

MAGNITUDE: The measure of brightness of stars.

METEORITE: A meteor that reaches the Earth's surface.

NEBULA:	A cloud of interstellar gas and/or dust.
NEUTRON STAR:	A small but extremely dense star made of neutrons. They are formed when the core of a supernova is compressed, crushing negatively charged electrons into positive protons to form neutral neutrons. If the body is too massive, neutron pressure is overcome and the star collapses further into a black hole.
OPEN CLUSTER:	A cluster of hundreds of stars lying in the plane of the galaxy.
PLANET:	A large body of solid and/or liquid matter that orbits a star but is not massive enough to become a star.
PLASMA THEORY:	A new theory that best explains the structure of the universe as being due to the forces of electricity, magnetism and gravity.
PULSAR:	A rapidly spinning neutron star that emits radio waves in a beam-like fashion.
QUASARS:	Starlike objects that appear to be very distant. They appear to be extremely active cores of galaxies possibly containing super-massive black holes.
SEEING:	A term used to describe the degree of atmospheric turbulence.
SHOOTING STAR:	A meteor — a small stone micro-asteroid burning up as it enters the Earth's atmosphere.
SOLAR SYSTEM:	A sun and its family of planets, moons, asteroids and comets etc. Such systems often have more than one sun involved.
STAR:	A very massive ball of predominately hydrogen and helium gas held together by gravity. The matter is so dense at the centre that atomic fusion occurs.
SUNSPOT:	Dark spots on the sun caused by magnetic storms.
SUPERGIANTS:	The largest and brightest stars known.
TERMINATOR:	The boundary on the surface of a planet or moon between the day side and the night side.
WHITE DWARF:	A small dim star in the final stages of its life.
ZENITH:	The point directly overhead.
ZODIACAL LIGHT:	Sunlight scattered by interplanetary dust in the plane of the solar system.

INDEX

LIST OF COLOUR PLATES

DRAWING FORM

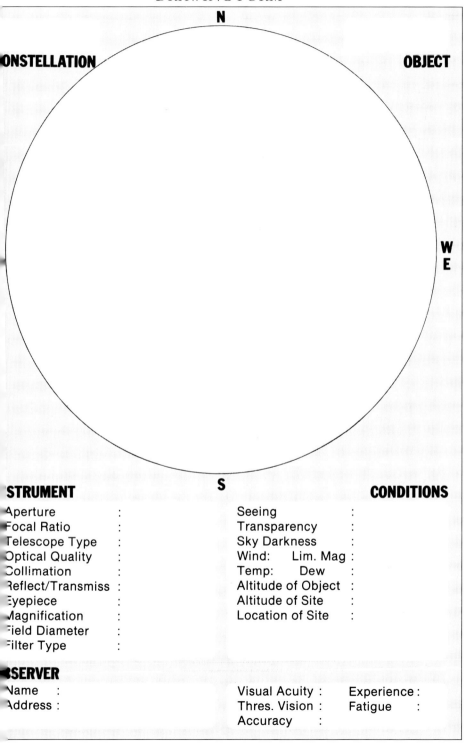

ONSTELLATION

OBJECT

N

S

W
E

STRUMENT

Aperture :
Focal Ratio :
Telescope Type :
Optical Quality :
Collimation :
Reflect/Transmiss :
Eyepiece :
Magnification :
Field Diameter :
Filter Type :

CONDITIONS

Seeing :
Transparency :
Sky Darkness :
Wind: Lim. Mag :
Temp: Dew :
Altitude of Object :
Altitude of Site :
Location of Site :

SERVER

Name :
Address :

Visual Acuity :   Experience :
Thres. Vision :   Fatigue :
Accuracy :

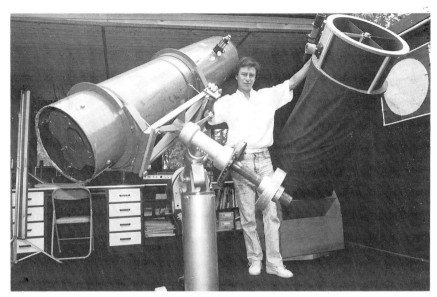

The author in his Springwood Observatory, south of Brisbane, with a 32cm f5.3 reflector and a portable 46cm f4.5 Dobsonian. The observatory features a special Dual Split Roof design which provides maximum utility yet is low in cost. The slit runs east–west and can be opened to accommodate full sky visibility when required. Photo: GD Thompson

Expert Australian astrophotographer, Steve Quirk sits inside Mudgee Observatory at the controls of his 25cm Newtonian reflector. The observatory now sports the heavy-duty 32cm telescope pictured above. Many fine examples of Steve's work appear in this book. Photo: S Quirk